Pastor Degorl shows readers the reality, the role, and the response we should all have to conquer our enemies. In order to live an abundant life, one needs to know what and who our enemy is. *Unveiling the Truth Behind Curses* is one of the most explained and detailed books I have read so far on the subject of curses. Degorl is right, and believers should stand on their authority of and promises in God's Word. This subject is almost forgotten in the body of Christ, and I am glad Pastor Degorl is bringing it back. It is a much needed and great focus on the authority of a child of the Most High God. Degorl not only shows the reader the causes but he also shows the way out in Jesus Christ. This book will help you find strength for today, and hope for tomorrow. A must read.

—CHRIS K. WILMOT
PRESIDENT AND CHIEF EXECUTIVE OFFICER,
WCW INTERNATIONAL, INC.
CHAIRMAN 2004–2005,
GREATER HOUSTON CONVENTION & VISITORS BUREAU
CHAIRMAN 2012–2013, WORLD TRADE BOARD,
GREATER HOUSTON PARTNERSHIP

In this book the truth behind curses is unveiled. But by the time you finish reading it, you will also know clearly how to cancel curses. So in one book Pastor Degorl deals with all the aspects of curses and how to overcome them. It's interesting how he takes the different curses and deals with their nature, manifestation, and how to cancel them. This book brings it all together beautifully. We are engaged in spiritual warfare and each believer has to understand and know how to fight. I recommend this book, *Unveiling the Truth Behind Curses*, to all believers. It will enrich your lives!

—MRS. MATILDA AMISSAH-ARTHUR
WIFE OF THE VICE PRESIDENT OF THE REPUBLIC OF GHANA
SENIOR ELDER OF ASBURY DUNWELL CHURCH, ACCRA, GHANA

Am excited to endorse Augustine Degorl's new book, *Unveiling the Truth Behind Curses*. There is a tremendous need in the church today for freedom from bondages that ruin the effectiveness of God's people. The Western church has been particularly lacking both in understanding and empowerment concerning the area of deliverance. Augustine's rich heritage in setting captives free qualifies him to explain the workings of the satanic realm. Our African brothers have a greater grasp of these truths than we in the Western church world, where the enemy is rarely confronted and often continues his wicked work undetected and unhindered. The importance of this book is the unraveling of the mystery of curses so the chains can be broken and the captives set free. The reader is not left with questions about how to make application of these powerful truths. Augustine reveals the causes and the remedies. Discovering the truth about where a curse comes from reveals the spiritual weaponry that should be used to break the curse. I highly recommend this clear and concise presentation concerning overcoming curses, written by a seasoned prayer warrior whose experience authenticates the, dynamic truths in the book.

—DR. SUE CURRAN
FOUNDER AND PASTOR, SHEKINAH CHURCH,
BLOUNTVILLE, TN

UNVEILING
THE TRUTH
BEHIND CURSES

AUGUSTINE DEGORL

CREATION
HOUSE

UNVEILING THE TRUTH BEHIND CURSES by Augustine Degorl
Published by Creation House
A Charisma Media Company
600 Rinehart Road
Lake Mary, Florida 32746
www.charismamedia.com

Unless otherwise noted, all Scripture quotations are from the King James Version of the Bible.

Scripture quotations marked AMP are from the Amplified Bible. Old Testament copyright © 1965, 1987 by the Zondervan Corporation. The Amplified New Testament copyright © 1954, 1958, 1987 by the Lockman Foundation. Used by permission.

Scripture quotations marked NIV are from the Holy Bible, New International Version. Copyright © 1973, 1978, 1984, 2010, 2011, International Bible Society. Used by permission.

Scripture quotations marked NKJV are from the New King James Version of the Bible. Copyright © 1979, 1980, 1982 by Thomas Nelson, Inc., publishers. Used by permission.

Design Director: Justin Evans
Cover design by Judy McKittrick Wright

Visit the author's website: www.augustinedegorlministries.org.

Library of Congress CataloginginPublication Data: 2014948489
International Standard Book Number: 978-1-62136-791-8
E-book International Standard Book Number: 978-1-62136-792-5

While the author has made every effort to provide accurate telephone numbers and Internet addresses at the time of publication, neither the publisher nor the author assumes any responsibility for errors or for changes that occur after publication.

First edition

14 15 16 17 18 — 987654321
Printed in Canada

This book is dedicated to my loving family: Lady Pat, my wife of twenty-two years; my two children, Austin Jr. and Chelsea. You have supported me and loved me unconditionally and have been a source of encouragement and inspiration. I'm eternally grateful to God for considering and counting me worthy to be a steward over you.

And, to my mentor and father, the Archbishop Duncan Williams, for the volumes of rich priceless life lessons and deposits of deep wells of knowledge and spiritual impartations; you are a true coach indeed.

CONTENTS

FOREWORD

KING DAVID KNEW the power and authority given to the king. He walked in that authority and wielded the power over his enemies. He not only fought opposing armies but opposing spirits throughout his reign.

We know we are kings and priests and have been given kingdom power and authority over all power of the enemy. Our authority is not limited by any means to any given situation. Once the spirit's identity is unveiled; we decree, declare, take authority, and dismiss the assignment of that enemy.

In this modern age, ancient spirits are rising again over nations, regions, states, and cities to try and breach the wall of faith and authority. These ancients are the same as were around in the days of the Old Testament prophets and after Christ's birth. Their assignment is still to discredit, weaken, and dislodge this kingdom generation.

Dr. Degorl has left no stone unturned in bringing this great revelation to the forefront for the believer. It is revolutionary and faith building. This book is an incredible tool that will bring a new level of victory to those struggling with unseen forces.

What becomes revelation to us brings restoration. Home run, my brother!

—ARCHBISHOP GENERAL DR. LAWRENCE LANGSTON
ARCHBISHOP GENERAL, TRANS-ATLANTIC
AND PACIFIC ALLIANCE OF CHURCHES
PRESIDENT OF TABERNACLE BIBLE COLLEGE AND SEMINARY
AND CHRISTIAN UNIVERSITY
TAMPA, FLORIDA, USA

ACKNOWLEDGEMENTS

THERE ARE A number of gracious and wonderful people whom God has used in many ways to be a source of inspiration to my life; their encouragement cannot be overlooked as it has contributed to my experience in writing this book.

I will always be grateful to my family for loaning me out graciously and patiently and in countless ways made significant contributions to making this manuscript a success story.

Lady Pat; your grace for patience and endurance never ceases to amaze me. The many nights you stayed up late to help me with typing and researching the Scriptures, including all the pieces of advice, have not been in vain. Most importantly the revelation of God that you shared with me makes you one of a kind and I am eternally grateful.

Archbishop Duncan Williams, my father in the Lord; my life has been greatly transformed with my feet firmly planted on the path of knowledge under your watch. You are an amazing mentor and a true general indeed.

Aunty Tilly; your busy schedule as the Second Lady of Ghana did not stop you from graciously taking time to guide me through the writing process and editing the manuscript. You are indeed an exceptional woman, a true God-sent dream helper and a destiny pusher. Thank you.

Allen Quain and the team at Creation House; thank you for believing in my dream and for taking on this project.

I also want to acknowledge the help constantly provided me by and from my church family.

A big thank you goes to Perinza Cornwell, who typed much of the manuscript.

Pastor Sue Curran of Shekinah Church; your invaluable advice and guidance on how to package a quality material for God's glory are appreciated.

Joseph Daniels, my brother-in-law, friend, and partner in ministry as well as associate pastor; you are always a source of encouragement to me, in prayer and God's Word.

Marian Asamoah-Anim; thank you for all your help, including the idea of the title of this book.

Prophet Victor Boateng; you are my covenant brother indeed. May God's abundance be made richly manifest in you to fulfill your purpose in Him.

Deep gratitude goes to my friends and partners who have stood by me and encouraged me to finish this project. Chris Wilmot, Joe and Carol Lopez, Ronnie Geahart, Will and Jennifer Ohrt, Linda and Carl Ampah, Esther and Mr. T; your prayers have helped me to complete this project.

My Friend and Helper the Holy Spirit; a special thank You is offered. I could not have come this far without You. Thank You for honoring Jesus in my life and for teaching me through the Word to love Him. By providing the grace and illumination of understanding the Scriptures You bestowed upon me, this assignment has become a reality.

INTRODUCTION

MY GOAL IN this book is to inspire you to rise and see yourself in the light of the Scriptures. Curses are real, but so also is the blessing. The good news is the force of the blessing cancels any curse and breaks it from our lives and bloodline.

Through disobedience, the first Adam lost the blessing and brought a curse upon himself and then to all mankind.

> For just as through the disobedience of the one man the many were made sinners, so also through the obedience of the one man the many will be made righteous.
> —ROMANS 5:19, NIV

Jesus Christ, the second Adam, walked in total submission and obedience to His Father; and by so doing, He broke the original curse and restored the blessing back unto all men. He also reconciled us back unto God. Obedience has always been the requirement by God in order for us to walk in the blessing and not the curses.

Under the old covenant, God spoke through Moses about how to maintain the blessing and avoid the curse:

> If you fully obey the LORD your God and carefully follow all his commands I give you today, the LORD your God will set you high above all the nations on earth. All these blessings will come on you and accompany you if you obey the LORD your God. You will be blessed in the city and blessed in the country.
> —DEUTERONOMY 28:1–3, NIV

The children of Israel inherited the curses when they disobeyed God's revealed word:

> Do not turn aside from any of the commands I give you today, to the right or to the left, following other gods and serving them.

However, if you do not obey the Lord your God and do not carefully follow all his commands and decrees I am giving you today,
all these curses will come on you and overtake you.

—Deuteronomy 28:14–15, niv

Jesus told His disciples to walk in 100 percent obedience to benefit
from the 100 percent blessings.

If you keep my commands, you will remain in my love, just as I
have kept my Father's commands and remain in his love... You
are my friends if you do what I command.

—John 15:10, 14, niv

Without exception, every one that God blessed throughout the history of humanity was and is as a result of their willingness to walk in
obedience. A curse must have a cause to prevail.

As the bird by wandering, as the swallow by flying, so the curse
causeless shall not come.

—Proverbs 26:2

For every curse that people experience in life, there is a cause. By
the grace of God, you will discover the root cause of the curse that has
plagued your bloodline and held you captive. God placed this book
in your hands to shed light on the subject of curses and blessings to
expose the hidden works of darkness.

You cannot recover what you have not discovered. This book
exposes the lies of the enemy and gives you the necessary knowledge
to break the curse and liberate your family. It is time to tell every servant sitting on your horse to get off.

I have seen servants upon horses, and princes walking as servants upon the earth.

—Ecclesiastes 10:7

It is time to uproot every ugly root and plant of generational curse
out of your life and bloodline.

He replied, "Every plant that my heavenly Father has not planted
will be pulled up by the roots."

—Matthew 15:13, niv

It is time to let the devil know enough is enough. You are a repairer, a restorer, and a builder according to Isaiah 58:12. Rise to the occasion and fight for what you desire and believe, put up a strong fight and don't relent. God has not promised you any defeats, only victories. The destiny and glorious future of your bloodline is in the balance, and you have the power right now to overturn the captivity and every curse into a blessing. You can do it because,

Greater is he that is in you, than he that is in the world.

—1 JOHN 4:4

PART I:
CAUSES AND EFFECTS

*Like the sparrow in her wandering, like the swallow in
her flying, so the causeless curse does not alight.*
[PROVERBS 26:2, AMP]

*How can I curse those God has not cursed? Or how can I [vio-
lently] denounce those the Lord has not denounced?*
[NUMBERS 23:8, AMP]

Chapter 1
NO CURSE WITHOUT A CAUSE

*Like the sparrow in her wandering, like the swallow in
her flying, so the causeless curse does not alight.*
—PROVERBS 26:2, AMP

F OR EVERY CURSE *that people experience in life, there is a cause.
Discovery precedes recovery.*

Until you discover the root cause of the curse and apply the
necessary force to break it, it remains in your bloodline for many
generations.

1. A person living under an unbroken curse may be a
    devout Christian, one who has given everything to serve
    the Lord, is very faithful in church, supports missions
    with his tithes and offerings, is present at every prayer
    gathering, and contributes during Bible study. He does
    all the right things. He may acquire several skills in
    business and work hard, perhaps even being ordained as
    a pastor with all the titles behind and before his name.

    Yet success eludes him. He cries out, "It is well!"
    behind the mask of pain and disappointment, frustra-
    tion and total failure. He claims scriptures, such as that
    he is a joint-heir with Christ (Rom. 8:17).

2. He knows that his place is at the Master's table to enjoy
    the bread fit for children, and yet his portion has always
    been the crumbs offered to dogs: "Truth, Lord: yet the
    dogs eat of the crumbs which fall from their masters'
    table" (Matt. 15:27).

    Robbed of inner peace and the joy of salvation, his
    marriage, maybe his family and his children are rebel-
    lious. Everything seems very gloom and life seems

meaningless because he has tried to rise time and again from the ashes of despair and failed. He feels tired of struggling and wrestling with everything, including his health, his purpose, and destiny. He feels haunted by a sense of unavailable love and failure. He sees others flourishing around him, including those he may have helped. He may have read and comforted himself with Psalm 1:2–3:

> But his delight is in the law of the Lord; and in his law doth he meditate day and season; his leaf also shall not wither; and whatsoever he doeth shall prosper.

His life is a cycle of "near success syndrome," always trying and never achieving success or victory. Whenever his door of opportunity seems to open, the enemy shuts it back in his face and positions strongmen to guard it.

3. This believer may be in a deep state of confusion, depression, and distress. He is now ready to throw in the towel. Some backslide at this stage; others give up the fight and blame God for everything. He never ceases to question God, "Why? Why me? Why have you not answered my prayers? Why have you not delivered me?" and so forth.

Like the psalmist he declares:

> My soul thirsteth for God, for the living God: when shall I come and appear before God? My tears have been my meat day and night, while they continually say unto me, Where is thy God? When I remember these things, I pour out my soul in me: for I had gone with the multitude, I went with them to the house of God, with the voice of joy and praise, with a multitude that kept holyday. Why art thou cast down, O my soul? And why art thou disquieted in me? Hope thou in God: for I shall yet praise him for the help of his countenance.
>
> —Psalm 42:2–5

The son of Korah encouraged himself to put his trust in God even though all was not well. He was a worship leader in the days of David the king and led many into worship before the Lord. While hiding his inner struggle and battle, it is clear from his prayer that he was fighting an unseen battle, with dark shadows and unseen forces constantly denying him of the promises of God and the blessings of Abraham. The testimony of Korah was the inevitable truth of Ecclesiastes 10:7: "I have seen servants upon horses, and princes walking as servants upon the earth."

The son of Korah never understood his battle; but as mentioned earlier, there was a "cause," there is a reason and a cause for every curse. "As the bird by wandering, as the swallow by flying, so the curse causeless shall not come" (Prov. 26:2).

The one word that sums up the effects of a curse is frustration. Frustration is a spirit driven by forces that are not completely subject to the usual laws of nature.

The assignment of these forces is to enforce the curse. They have the same effect on nations, cities, villages, families, and individuals.

By now you're beginning to identify with the truth of this book. God placed it in your hands because it is in line with His plan for your life; and you will discover the antidote, a remedy to breaking every curse out of your life. Jesus said, "Every plant, which my heavenly Father hath not planted, shall be rooted up" (Matt. 15:13).

I see every curse in your life broken and uprooted right now by the Spirit of the breaker in the mighty name of Jesus!

> Even today is my complaint bitter: my stroke is heavier than my groaning. Oh that I knew where I might find him! that I might come even to his seat! I would order my cause before him, and fill my mouth with arguments. I would know the words which he would answer me, and understand what he would say unto me.
>
> —JOB 23:2–5

> For he shall be like the heath in the desert, and shall not see when good cometh; but shall inhabit the parched places in the wilderness, in a salt land and not inhabited.
>
> —JEREMIAH 17:6

ZEAL WITHOUT KNOWLEDGE

Most curses in life are self-inflicted because of lack of knowledge. Through youthful exuberance and being ignorant of the spirit realm, many believers have inflicted and heaped curses upon themselves that will eventually have a ripple effect even on generations yet unborn unless they are discovered and broken.

> My people are destroyed from lack of knowledge. Because you have rejected knowledge, I also reject you as my priests; because you have ignored the law of your God, I also will ignore your children.
>
> —HOSEA 4:6, NIV

God spoke through His prophet Jeremiah:

> For my people have committed two evils; they have forsaken me the fountain of living waters, and hewed them out cisterns, broken cisterns, that can hold no water. Is Israel a servant? Is he a home-born slave? why is he spoiled?...Hast thou not procured this unto thyself, in that thou hast forsaken the LORD thy God, when he led thee by the way?
>
> —JEREMIAH 2:13–14, 17

Many believers hide behind positive confession and quote all the scriptures on the promises of God for many years without seeing any results. They declare "all is well" when all is not well. They quote:

> The LORD will make you the head, not the tail. If you pay attention to the commands of the LORD your God that I give you this day and carefully follow them, you will always be at the top, never at the bottom.
>
> —DEUTERONOMY 28:13, NIV

They can see that the previous generation went through the same cycle and struggle. Nobody seems to rise above average. Psalm 109:10 is a perfect picture of the family and bloodline: "Let his children be continually vagabonds, and beg: let them seek their bread also out of their desolate places."

Life seems to deal them a deadly blow; they hop from one business to another, encroaching on others as they go along in life because of the difficulties and cares of life. They tiptoe and hop between the church and the world.

The men in these families take out their frustrations on their wives and children; they eventually resign to alcohol and gambling, confused and not finding the right job to do. Oftentimes they may rise and enjoy some level of successes briefly in their early years only to lose it all through unforeseen calamities. The women also either struggle or are frustrated in marriage or don't marry at all. They may be well educated, probably the prettiest in their communities, and yet they are unable to sustain relationships and marriage. Is there any possibility that a "generational curse" is operational in such families?

Look at this scripture: "Lest Satan should get an advantage of us: for we are not ignorant of his devices. (2 Cor. 2:11). The advantage of Satan over anybody is due to their ignorance. Jesus said, "And ye shall know the truth, and the truth shall make you free" (John 8:32).

The answers and remedy to these questions and problems begins with you.

YOUR GREATEST ENEMY

The prophet Isaiah declared, "Therefore my people are gone into captivity, because they have no knowledge: and their honourable men are famished, and their multitude dried up with thirst" (Isa. 5:13).

God spoke through his prophet Haggai:

> Now this is what the LORD Almighty says: "Give careful thought to your ways. You have planted much, but harvested little. You eat, but never have enough. You drink, but never have your fill. You put on clothes, but are not warm. You earn wages, only to put them in a purse with holes in it." This is what the LORD Almighty says: "Give careful thought to your ways."
>
> —HAGGAI 1:5–7, NIV

Jesus said, "And a man's foes shall be they of his own household" (Matt. 10:36). The majority of believers read the above scripture and immediately apportion blame to close relatives like brothers, sisters, cousins, uncles, and the list goes on. A closer study of this scripture together with other scriptures reveals that *we* may possibly be our worst enemy.

Proverbs 6:16–17 sheds much light on this truth: "There are six things the LORD hates, seven that are detestable to him: haughty eyes, a lying tongue, hands that shed innocent blood" (NIV).

Ephesians 4:27 tells us: "Neither give place to the devil."

Colossians 3:5 is specific: "Mortify therefore your members which are upon the earth; fornication, uncleanness, inordinate affection, evil concupiscence, and covetousness, which is idolatry."

It is easier to blame everybody else for the problems and challenges we face in life, but the above scriptures point to the man in the mirror to change his ways and come into divine alignment with the Word of God. It is worthy to note that the Bible recognizes two enemies: yourself and Satan.

Let us consider other scriptures. Haggai 1:7 clearly admonishes us to "give careful thought to your ways" (NIV). The prophet Haggai's generation was not living in the fullness of God's blessings. They labored hard, but had very little to show in the season of harvest. God sent Haggai (whose name means "festival") to destroy the yoke and stigma of mediocrity and restore the people back to God's original plan and the Abrahamic blessing.

The remnant of the Jews that returned from the Babylonian captivity were selfish, preoccupied with building their houses and personal gain rather than rebuilding the Lord's temple. They brought down divine curses on their generation.

> Therefore the heaven over you is stayed from dew, and the earth is stayed from her fruit. And I called for a drought upon the land, and upon the mountains, and upon the corn, and upon the new wine, and upon the oil, and upon that which the ground bringeth forth, and upon men, and upon cattle, and upon all the labor of the hands.
> —HAGGAI 1:10–11

Due to advancement in this modern age of information, many believers make light of these teachings as fit for third world countries. Many quickly acknowledge and accept the blessings while ignoring the reality of the curses plaguing them and tearing them apart. This teaching sounds too shallow to some and offends the intellectual dispositions of others. We hide behind a mask, makeup, and a veil. It is time to take the mask off and assume our place of authority to fulfill the purpose for which God placed this book in your hands.

> And they that shall be of thee shall *build* the old waste places: thou shalt raise up the foundations of many generations; and thou shalt be called, The *repairer* of the breach, The *restorer* of paths to dwell in.
> —ISAIAH 58:12, EMPHASIS ADDED

God calls you "builder, repairer, and restorer!" Receive it in Jesus' name!

Your generation will be the devil's last stop. He will not be able to visit these curses on the next generation because you will rise and stop him. Now is the time. Now is the hour. Jesus said, "The hour cometh, and now is" (John 4:23a), and, "…lift up your heads; for your redemption draweth nigh" (Luke 21:28b).

Arise, take up your weapons of war, and run into the battle to deliver yourself and the next generation. Much is dependent on you acquiring knowledge, which is light and illumination. Don't allow pride, arrogance, and the sense of false security to prevent you from breaking the curses on your life and laying a good foundation for future generations to stand upon.

All your life you've struggled and fought against something amorphous and elusive, dark shadows, unseen forces behind the scene; things you can't lay your finger on or identify. You have come close to throwing in the towel and giving up many, many times. Success seems to have eluded you on every side, in every endeavor, in everything, and everywhere. Time and again you have cried yourself to bed and oftentimes suffered sleepless nights seeking for answers. "What's the use?" you may have exclaimed. "Nothing ever goes right for me!" You may even take the easy way out by seeking death to end it all as others have done—rich and poor, young and old, male and female. A curse has no respect for gender; it does not discriminate against race. It does not care where you come from and what nationality you belong to. Until you arise to discover the root cause, you cannot recover from it; and the generation after you may even pay a heavier price for the battles you refused to fight: "Who knoweth whether thou art come to the kingdom for such a time as this?" (Esther 4:14b).

Computer technology has made it easy to trace our roots and to know who our ancestors were and what battles they fought and whether there were similarities of repeated cycles of failure, abuse, and struggles close to your struggles. A close study of your background could reveal an unbroken curse operating in the bloodline.

The Bible says,

> Hearken to me, ye that follow after righteousness, ye that seek the LORD: look unto the rock whence ye are hewn, and to the hole of the pit whence ye are digged. Look unto Abraham your father, and unto Sarah that bare you: for I called him alone, and blessed him, and increased him.
> —ISAIAH 51:1–2

It might be worthwhile at this point to take a break and prayerfully research and know your ancestors and background to give you a clear picture of what you are up against.

Abraham and his wife Sarah were the first Hebrews and Jews:

> And there came one that had escaped, and told Abram the Hebrew; for he dwelt in the plain of Mamre the Amorite, brother of Eshcol, and brother of Aner: and these were confederate with Abram.
> —GENESIS 14:13

God asked His people to look back to their roots. A curse could stretch back many generations or it could start with you. Either way, it is worth searching to know the cause and the appropriate steps to take to break it. This is not the hour to blame others and point fingers. The good news is the Holy Spirit through this book is shedding light on the subject and is also empowering you even now with His ability to break every curse and be liberated.

There are several behind-the-scenes forces whose singular assignment is to enforce the curse, to make sure you don't rise or lift up your head.

Consider this story in the Book of Daniel:

> Then said he unto me, Fear not, Daniel: for from the first day that thou didst set thine heart to understand and to chasten thyself before thy God, thy words were heard, and I am come for thy words. But the prince of the kingdom of Persia withstood me one

and twenty days: but, lo, Michael, one of the chief princes, came to help me; and I remained there with the kings of Persia.

—DANIEL 10:12–13

Daniel was hindered for twenty-one days, but his persistency and determination paid off when heaven sent reinforcement in the person of Michael the archangel.

Then lifted I up mine eyes, and saw, and behold four horns. And I said unto the angel that talked with me, What be these? And he answered me, These are the horns which have scattered Judah, Israel, and Jerusalem.

—ZECHARIAH 1:18–19

The above scriptures clearly show that there are spiritual forces—spirits familiar with your bloodline (familiar spirits)—wicked forces positioned by the devil to prevent your victory, success, and your breakthroughs. They fight your progress and block the rains from reaching your soil. But there is hope and good news through the testimony of Jesus Christ.

And the LORD shewed me four carpenters. Then said I, What come these to do? And he spake, saying, These are the horns which have scattered Judah, so that no man did lift up his head: but these are come to fray them, to cast out the horns of the Gentiles, which lifted up their horn over the land of Judah to scatter it.

—ZECHARIAH 1:20–21

Don't give up fighting the good fight of faith. Press your way to victory. You have come too far to quit.

You can win "because greater is he that is in you, than he that is in the world" (1 John 4:4b), and, "for they that be with us are more than they that be with them" (2 Kings 6:16b).

*Death and life are in the power of the tongue, and they who
indulge in it shall eat the fruit of it [for death or life].*
[PROVERBS 18:21, AMP]

*For by your words you will be justified and acquitted, and
by your words you will be condemned and sentenced.*
[MATTHEW 12:37, AMP]

Chapter 2
OPERATIONAL MEDIUM OF A CURSE

A CURSE IS DEFINED as a solemn utterance to invoke a supernatural power to inflict harm or punishment on someone or something. Dictionary.com defines a curse as "the expression of a wish that misfortune, evil, doom, etc., befall a person, group, etc.[1] In his book, *Blessings and Curses*, Derek Prince says,

> A curse could also be likened to a long, evil arm stretched out from the past. It rest upon you with a dark, oppressive force that inhibits the full expression of your personality. You never feel completely free to be yourself. You sense that you have potential that is never fully developed. You always expect more of yourself than you are able to achieve, or again, that long, evil arm may have the effect of tripping you as you walk. Your way seems clear before you; but from time to time you stumble, yet you cannot see what it was you stumbled over. For some uncanny reason, the moments at which you stumble are those when you are within reach of attaining some long sought goal. Yet your goal eludes you. Actually the word "uncanny" could be likened to a red warning light. You experience events or situations for which you can find no natural or logical reason. It seems that there is some force at work that is not completely subject to the usual laws of nature or of averages.[2]

Let's look at another definition quoted by George Hartwell: "A curse is sometimes defined as 'the invocation of supernatural power to inflict harm upon someone or something.'"[3] He goes on to define a curse as,

> The harmful energy released against by the use of witchcraft, hateful words, slander by one's hateful attitude and by negative and even, controlling or witchcraft prayer by a Christian. Hearing and not refusing a message from a psychic, gypsy, or

fortune teller acts the same way. A negative diagnosis by a medical doctor, a negative prediction by a school guidance teacher,
taunts by your peers, things, said during discipline by your parents, any and all of these can and do act as curses.[4]

All these definitions and quotes point to the fact that all curses have
a root cause. They operate in the realm of the spirit and manifest or
have their effect in the natural by the spirit of the demonic enforcer or
familiar spirit assigned against the individual, family, thing, or place.

*Curses that operate against you as a result of the previous genera-
tion or fathers are known as generational curses.*

In dealing with generational curses, you cannot explain to the forces
of darkness that *you were not there.* A study of your ancestors will
enlighten you about what you are dealing with, and then knowledge of
God's Word and knowing who you are in Christ gives you the authority
and know how to deal with these curses, "because greater is he that is
in you, than he that is in the world" (1 John 4:4b).

THE TONGUE

*There are many sources by which curses come upon an individual. At
the top is the creative force within our tongue.*

Death and life are in the power of the tongue.
—PROVERBS 18:21A

Words are very powerful because the Creator made it so. He created
us in His image and likeness, and He has deposited within our *lips* the
force to create with our words. Every time you open your mouth, you
are either speaking life or death, creating or destroying, blessing or
cursing. Those who understand and appreciate the creative force of the
tongue carefully channel their words to create and bless not only themselves but everything and everyone around them.

Consider this scripture "How forcible are right words" (Job 6:25a).
Right words come from God and have the potency to change your
world: "For by thy words thou shalt be justified, and by thy words
thou shalt be condemned" (Matt. 12:37).

Whereas the devil is the enforcer of negative words, God also is the
enforcer of positive words. You can talk and confess yourself out of

your possessions or you can declare and claim the promises of God by your words. We are all justified or condemned by our words.

> That confirmeth the word of his servant, and performeth the counsel of his messengers; that saith to Jerusalem, Thou shalt be inhabited; and to the cities of Judah, Ye shall be built, and I will raise up the decayed places thereof.
>
> —Isaiah 44:26

The children of Israel talked themselves out of their possession of the Promised Land at Kadesh Barnea. They limited God by their words by focusing on the size of their opponents. They said, "We be not able to go up against the people; for they are stronger than we" (Num. 13:31b). They saw the mighty works of God in Egypt, through the Red Sea, and in the conquest of Sihon the Amorite and Og king of Bashan. These were giants and God allowed these battles as a reference point for Israel. In response to their negative words, God also told them,

> How long shall I bear with this evil congregation, which murmur against me? I have heard the murmurings of the children of Israel, which they murmur against me. Say unto them, As truly as I live, saith the Lord, as ye have spoken in mine ears, so will I do to you.
>
> —Numbers 14:27–28

The eleven-day journey quickly became forty years. Wrong confessions will cost you your life, family, business, and everyone around you, for "death and life are in the power of the tongue" (Prov. 18:21).

Carefully consider these warnings from the Bible as to how the potency of words can affect you either positively or negatively, good or bad, blessings or curses:

> An hypocrite with his mouth destroyeth his neighbour: but through knowledge shall the just be delivered.
>
> —Proverbs 11:9

> There is that speaketh like the piercings of a sword: but the tongue of the wise is health.
>
> —Proverbs 12:18

A wholesome tongue is a tree of life: but perverseness therein is
a breach in the spirit.

—PROVERBS 15:4

And the LORD spake unto Moses and unto Aaron, saying, How
long shall I bear with this evil congregation, which murmur
against me? I have heard the murmurings of the children of
Israel, which they murmur against me. Say unto them, As truly
as I live, saith the LORD, as ye have spoken in mine ears, so will
I do to you.

—NUMBERS 14:26–28

A man shall eat good by the fruit of his mouth: but the soul of
the transgressors shall eat violence.

—PROVERBS 13:2

Isn't it time to put a guard on your lips? Most are quick to speak and
slow to listen, but it should be the other way around—quick to listen
and slow to speak. Take time to think your words through before letting them out. Refrain from the attitude of just letting your words out
there like hot cakes. The Bible says it can lead you to ruin. "Can a man
take fire in his bosom and his clothes not be burned?" (Prov. 6:27).
Surely you will be burned if you carry fire in your bosom.

The scripture is very plain and specific on the subject. "Thou art
snared with the words of thy mouth, thou art taken with the words
of thy mouth" (Prov. 6:2). You can be denied, trapped, ensnared, dis-
allowed, restricted, come to naught, by the words of your lips. In the
United States when the authorities arrest an individual, they read
him his rights; and part of that statement says, "You have the right to
remain silent."

Jesus said there is a day of accountability for every idle word we
utter: "But I say unto you, that every idle word that men shall speak,
they shall give account thereof in the day of judgment" (Matt. 12:36).
"The wicked is snared by the transgression of his lips" (Prov. 12:13a).

*Make no mistake about it, "Life and death, blessings and cursing,
are all in the power of your lips.*

Are you in any trouble because of your words? Are you in the habit
of constantly speaking negative to your circumstances, family, health,
business, etc.? It's time to put a guard on your lips.

Grace is being released and poured upon you right now to repent from the way you may have handled your God-given words casually. Power is being released and poured upon you even now to begin to cancel every idle and negative word you may have spoken over your circumstances, situation, family, spouse, children, friends, business, environment, bloodline, etc.

RECEIVE THE POWER NOW

The Bible declares, "But as many as received him, to them gave he power to become the sons of God, even to them that believe on his name" (John 1:12).

Consider this story in the New Testament in Luke 22:54–61: Peter sat by the fireplace, a fireplace set by the enemies of Jesus, and there he denied the Master three times. When Jesus rose from the dead, He got Peter and the others disciples to sit around another fireplace that He prepared; and there He gave Peter the chance to cancel his negative confession and denial of his Master three times (see John 21:9–17). The significance of this story is the fact that Jesus had taught His disciples, including Peter, that "whosoever shall deny me before men, him will I also deny before my Father which is in heaven" (Matt. 10:33); and, "He that denieth me before men shall be denied before the angels of God" (Luke 12:9).

Read the story in John 21:15–17:

> So when they had dined, Jesus saith to Simon Peter, Simon, son of Jonas, lovest thou me more than these? He saith unto him, Yea, Lord; thou knowest that I love thee. He saith unto him, Feed my lambs. He saith to him again the second time, Simon, son of Jonas, lovest thou me? He saith unto him, Yea, Lord; thou knowest that I love thee. He saith unto him, Feed my sheep. He saith unto him the third time, Simon, son of Jonas, lovest thou me? Peter was grieved because he said unto him the third time, Lovest thou me? And he said unto him, Lord, thou knowest all things; thou knowest that I love thee. Jesus saith unto him, Feed my sheep.

Which fireplace are you sitting at? Does it bring glory to God? Or do you deny Him because of those around? Are you able to speak positive words? Or do you compromise and join the so called "crowd" and "status quo" just to fit in?

Ten spies came back from spying out the land of promise; and by their negative perception and confession, they brought a curse upon an entire generation.

> And they returned from searching of the land after forty days. And they went and came to Moses, and to Aaron, and to all the congregation of the children of Israel, unto the wilderness of Paran, to Kadesh; and brought back word unto them, and unto all the congregation, and shewed them the fruit of the land. And they told him, and said, We came unto the land whither thou sentest us, and surely it floweth with milk and honey; and this is the fruit of it. Nevertheless the people be strong that dwell in the land and the cities are walled, and very great: and moreover we saw the children of Anak there. The Amalekites dwell in the land of the south: and the Hittites, and the Jebusites, and the Amorites, dwell in the mountains: and the Canaanites dwell by the sea, and by the coast of Jordan.
>
> —NUMBERS 13:25–29

Now listen to Caleb the son of Jephunneh and Joshua the son of Nun in verse 30: "And Caleb stilled the people before Moses, and said, Let us go up at once, and possess it; for we are well able to overcome it" (v. 30). The saga continued in verses 31–33, where evil rose up against good:

> But the men that went up with him said, We be not able to go up against the people; for they are stronger than we. And they brought up an evil report of the land which they had searched unto the children of Israel, saying, The land, through which we have gone to search it, is a land that eateth up the inhabitants thereof; and all the people that we saw in it are men of a great stature. And there we saw the giants, the sons of Anak, which come of the giants: and we were in our own sight as grasshoppers, and so we were in their sight.

Every time you cancel the curse and begin to speak the blessings, you will face opposition; especially among those you surround yourself with, by those closest to you.

But be strong and courageous, for "greater is he that is in you, than he that is in the world" (1 John 4:4b).

Words, whether negatively or positively spoken, will produce results (outcome). Let's go back to the Scriptures and examine the results of the negative confessions of the ten spies.

Read the entire chapter of Numbers 14. The promise and intent of God was to bring them into the land He promised Abraham, Isaac, and Jacob. He demonstrated His power in their deliverance from Egypt. He bore them on the wings of His angel as they traveled through the wilderness and enemy territory. He held back their enemies and separated the waters of the Red Sea, allowing them free passage into safety. They saw the army of Egypt drown to death, they ate angel's food, and He protected and led them by the pillar of cloud and fire. They heard His audible voice from heaven to affirm His continual presence.

But they kept limiting the Holy One of Israel. Ten spies brought an evil report that provoked a chain reaction of rebelliousness and murmuring against God and His anointed servant. They spoke death over the people. Their words cancelled the blessing that started with Abraham down through Joseph and then on to them. They spoke of their inability to posses the land because of their fear of the giants. God spoke to Moses in verses 27–30:

> How long will this wicked community grumble against me? I have heard the complaints of these grumbling Israelites. So tell them, 'As surely as I live, declares the LORD, I will do to you the very thing I heard you say: In this wilderness your bodies will fall—every one of you twenty years old or more who was counted in the census and who has grumbled against me. Not one of you will enter the land I swore with uplifted hand to make your home, except Caleb son of Jephunneh and Joshua son of Nun.
>
> —NUMBERS 14:27–30, NIV

> God is not a man, that he should lie; neither the son of man, that he should repent: hath he said, and shall he not do it? or hath he spoken, and shall he not make it good?
>
> —NUMBERS 23:19

For all the promises of God in him are yea, and in him Amen, unto the glory of God by us.

—2 CORINTHIANS 1:20

For whatsoever is born of God overcometh the world: and this is the victory that overcometh the world, even our faith.

—1 JOHN 5:4

God forbid: yea, let God be true, but every man a liar; as it is written, That thou mightest be justified in thy sayings, and mightest overcome when thou art judged.

—ROMANS 3:4

The tongue, according to the apostle James, is a small member of the body, but the hardest of all to control.

We all stumble in many ways. Anyone who is never at fault in what they say is perfect, able to keep their whole body in check. When we put bits into the mouths of horses to make them obey us, we can turn the whole animal. Or take ships as an example. Although they are so large and are driven by strong winds, they are steered by a very small rudder wherever the pilot wants to go. Likewise, the tongue is a small part of the body, but it makes great boasts. Consider what a great forest is set on fire by a small spark. The tongue also is a fire, a world of evil among the parts of the body. It corrupts the whole body, sets the whole course of one's life on fire, and is itself set on fire by hell. All kinds of animals, birds, reptiles and sea creatures are being tamed and have been tamed by mankind, but no human being can tame the tongue. It is a restless evil, full of deadly poison. With the tongue we praise our Lord and Father, and with it we curse human beings, who have been made in God's likeness. Out of the same mouth come praise and cursing. My brothers and sisters, this should not be.

—JAMES 3:2–10, NIV

Matthew 15:11 is a key scripture, shedding much light on how those careless words we let loose out of our lips damage us in the realm of the spirit before manifesting in the natural. "Not that which goeth into the mouth defileth a man; but that which cometh out of the mouth, this defileth a man."

Your life today is the product of those words you spoke yesterday; your tomorrow will be the product of what you speak and declare today.

Why not prophesy blessings into your life?

OTHER CHANNELS BY WHICH CURSES OR BLESSINGS MAY BE TRANSMITTED

Physical objects that we bring into our homes sometimes could carry a curse, and the deities to which these objects are dedicated come and lodge in our lives and place of residence. They take up territory and become territorial devils enforcing curses over the home or region. People who are souvenir lovers especially fall prey to this trap. They travel to distant shores and find objects sold at the open market and go to great lengths to bring these objects home and display them innocently and ignorantly on the walls of their homes and office. If these objects were dedicated to some god or used in some ritual, you may have subjected yourself, family, business, and loved ones to the curse of those gods and rituals.

Israel was doing fine in battle until Achan got greedy and decided to disobey the direct command of God by the mouth of His servant Joshua. Read the account of this tragedy in Joshua 7:1–26. As a leader in Israel and a family man, Achan's greed and sin rocked his family boat and brought great calamity to Israel. Israel suffered a great defeat in battle with about three thousand casualties. Achan stole some unclean things and brought them into his tent. His family paid a terrible price: they were stoned to death to remove the curse and break its effect from Israel.

As believers, we may never experience true victory until we have the victory over greed. Our dependency should be on Him by grace and not in our abilities.

Have you touched any accursed thing and is your family paying the price for your sins? Isn't it time you went through your house and office to get rid of every accursed thing? This includes demonic books, rings, necklaces, sculptures, psychic objects, demonic music, or ignorantly praying to dead relatives whereby invoking demonic and familiar spirits into your home and environment. If this will help, discuss with your pastor any things in your home or workplace that you are not sure about.

One of the last people King Saul of Israel spoke to before dying was the witch of Endor. He went in hope of speaking to Samuel who was already in the bosom of Abraham. A familiar spirit spoke to him in disguise pretending to be the spirit of Samuel. He then ate his lunch or dinner in the witch's bedchamber; He rose from there, went into battle, and died a horrible death. (See 1 Samuel 28:7–15.)

In Deuteronomy, time and again Moses warned Israel against any association with those nations that had sold themselves to idolatry.

> The graven images of their gods shall ye burn with fire: thou shalt not desire the silver or gold that is on them, nor take it unto thee, lest thou be snared therin: for it is an abomination to the LORD thy God. Neither shalt thou bring an abomination into thine house, lest thou be a cursed thing like it: but thou shalt utterly detest it, and thou shalt utterly abhor it; for it is a cursed thing.
> —DEUTERONOMY 7:25–26

God disowned these nations and allowed Israel to dispossess them and take over their nations.

The people you associate with can either help you up or bring you down. They could bring a curse into your life or blessings. The curse certainly will block the blessings. They can block your financial blessings, healing, education, spiritual growth, family, marriage, and ultimately cause you to fail in your journey into fulfilling purpose.

In the next few chapters, we will examine various types of curses, what opens the door to these curses, and ultimately how to break them. We will also look at how to access God's blessings to replace curses.

And I will bless those who bless you [who confer prosperity or happiness upon you] and curse him who curses or uses insolent language toward you; in you will all the families and kindred of the earth be blessed [and by you they will bless themselves].
[GENESIS 12:3, AMP]

Chapter 3

THE CURSE OF GOD

O NE WOULD ARGUE why a loving God who created us in His image and likeness would curse to begin with. Well let's look at the Genesis account:

> So the LORD God said to the serpent, "Because you have done this, Cursed are you above all livestock and all wild animals! You will crawl on your belly and you will eat dust all the days of your life. And I will put enmity between you and the woman, and between your offspring and hers; he will crush your head, and you will strike his heel." To the woman he said, "I will make your pains in childbearing very severe; with painful labor you will give birth to children. Your desire will be for your husband, and he will rule over you." To Adam he said, "Because you listened to your wife and ate fruit from the tree about which I commanded you, 'You must not eat from it,' Cursed is the ground because of you; through painful toil you will eat food from it all the days of your life. It will produce thorns and thistles for you and you will eat the plants of the field. By the sweat of your brow you will eat your food until you return to the ground, since from it you were taken; for dust you are and to dust you will return."
>
> —GENESIS 3:14–19, NIV

God promised Abraham, "I will bless them that bless thee, and curse him that curseth thee: and in thee shall all families of the earth be blessed" (Gen. 12:3).

THE FALL OF MAN

Our early parents brought a curse upon the human race. Without salvation, the ungodly remains under this curse.

How shall we escape, if we neglect so great salvation; which at
the first began to be spoken by the Lord, and was confirmed
unto us by them that heard him.

—HEBREWS 2:3

Until you are born again by accepting God's free gift of salvation,
you remain under the original curse, but God has made a way of
escape through Jesus Christ, His only begotten Son.

For God so loved the world, that he gave his only begotten Son,
that whosoever believeth in him should not perish, but have
everlasting life.

—JOHN 3:16

DISOBEDIENCE

The initial curse that passed from Adam unto all mankind came as a
result of disobedience. This is recorded in Genesis 3:14–19.

The first king of Israel ultimately lost his throne and was rejected
because of disobedience.

And Samuel said, Hath the LORD as great delight in burnt offerings and sacrifices, as in obeying the voice of the LORD? Behold, to
obey is better than sacrifice, and to hearken than the fat of rams.
For rebellion is as the sin of witchcraft, and stubbornness is as
iniquity and idolatry. Because thou hast rejected the word of the
LORD, he hath also rejected thee from being king.

—1 SAMUEL 15:22–23

"Willful disobedience" is what caused the downfall of mankind, and
the trend has never stopped. Throughout the Bible, willful disobedience
has rocked the boat of anybody that continued willfully in *sin*. It is what
will ultimately drive anybody into eternal damnation.

In Deuteronomy 28:15, Moses emphasized that the primary cause
of "all" curses is willful disobedience or rebellion against God. He
tabulated a comprehensive list of the various forms of blessings and
curses and how they operate. Take time to study the entire chapter of
Deuteronomy 28. Allow the great Teacher, the Holy Spirit, to guide and
teach you as you open the scriptures to Deuteronomy 28:1–68.

Obedience is the master key to escaping the curse and embracing the blessings.

God spoke to Israel through Moses at Mt. Sinai: "Now therefore, if ye will obey my voice indeed, and keep my covenant, then ye shall be a peculiar treasure unto me above all people: for all the earth is mine" (Exod. 19:5).

Jesus said "If ye love me, keep my commandments" (John 14:15).

Isn't it time to hear the voice of the Holy Spirit calling you into salvation?

God has never changed and will never change. "For I am the LORD, I change not" (Mal. 3:6). God *does not change.* But you and I can change by accepting His free gift of salvation through Jesus Christ.

Would you take a few moments and prayerfully accept Jesus as your Savior and break away from sin and disobedience? If you have not already done that, here is a great way to start.

Pray with me.

Dear Lord Jesus,

Thank You for dying in my place, paying the ultimate price to redeem me from sin. I renounce sin and accept You as my personal Lord and Savior. Wash away my sins and make me whole. Now, precious Holy Spirit, come and dwell in my heart teach me and guide me from today forward. I'm totally Yours, Lord. Thank You in Jesus' name. Amen.

STEALING AND SWEARING FALSELY

The Archbishop Duncan Williams once said, "Evil is never satisfied until good is destroyed."[1] This statement is a perfect picture of the flying scroll in Zechariah 5:

> I looked again, and there before me was a flying scroll. He asked me, "What do you see?" I answered, "I see a flying scroll, twenty cubits long and ten cubits wide." And he said to me, "This is the curse that is going out over the whole land; for according to what it says on one side, every thief will be banished, and according to what it says on the other, everyone who swears falsely will be banished. The LORD Almighty declares, 'I will send it out, and it will enter the house of the thief and the house of anyone who swears

falsely by my name. It will remain in that house and destroy it completely, both its timbers and its stones.'"

—ZECHARIAH 5:1, NIV

The prophet saw a vision of God's curse entering the home of those who swear falsely and also steal God's money! You might ask how can anyone swear falsely or steal from God. Well, let's go to the Scriptures for understanding.

Will a man rob God? Yet ye have robbed me. But ye say, Wherein have we robbed thee? In tithes and offerings. Ye are cursed with a curse: for ye have robbed me, even this whole nation.

—MALACHI 3:8–9

This scripture points out the fact that God keeps record of our tithes and offerings to break the curse on your money. God admonishes all believers of every generation in Malachi 3:10:

Bring ye all the tithes into the storehouse, that there may be meat in mine house, and prove me now herewith, saith the LORD of hosts, if I will not open you the windows of heaven, and pour you out a blessing, that there shall not be room enough to receive it.

—MALACHI 3:10

Two things are required by God to break the curse and reap the blessings, these also transcend every generation. The requirements are *repentance* and *restitution*.

Let's consider two examples one from the Old Testament and another from the New Testament.

Is it time for you, O ye, to dwell in your ceiled houses, and this house lie waste? Now therefore thus saith the LORD of hosts; Consider your ways. Ye have sown much, and bring in little; ye eat, but ye have not enough; ye drink, but ye are not filled with drink; ye clothe you, but there is none warm; and he that earneth wages earneth wages to put it into a bag with holes.

—HAGGAI 1:4–6

The remnant of Israel that returned from captivity to the land of promise, quickly forgot about the house of God. Their attitude was "to each his own," as they focused on their own homes and family while the house of the Lord lay in ruin.

They consistently robbed God by withholding their tithes and offerings. This was greed and selfishness. God sent His prophet Haggai to pull back the curtain and show them the curse that was eating away their harvest and increase.

Are you working hard and yet have nothing to show for your labor? Have you pondered why all the blessings that have passed through your hands have vanished into thin air? Could you possibly be dealing with an invincible hand, behind-the-scenes forces eating away at your harvest and increase?

You may be dealing with a curse. Remember, evil is never satisfied until good is completely destroyed—the flying scroll of Zechariah 5 that enters the house of the thief and liar will not leave until every good is completely destroyed. The prophets Malachi, Haggai, and Zechariah all require first repentance and secondly restitution in order to be restored and to stop the devourer.

> That which the palmerworm hath left hath the locust eaten; and that which the locust hath left hath the cankerworm eaten; and that which the cankerworm hath left hath the caterpillar eaten.
>
> —JOEL 1:4

Locust, cankerworms, and caterpillars are devourers; but restitution will deliver you into the realm of restoration as recorded in Joel 2:25: "And I will restore to you the years that the locust hath eaten, the cankerworm, and the caterpillar, and the palmerworm, my great army which I sent among you."

Now let's consider the New Testament example of Zacchaeus the tax collector. Zacchaeus was a man who cared nothing for God or his own people; he defrauded them to enrich himself, though he was a Jew. He worked for the Roman government as a tax collector. He admitted to Jesus after their encounter that he had lied, cheated, and defrauded his own people. But when he repented before Jesus publicly and decided to make restitution, immediately Jesus told him salvation had come to his house. This encounter is recorded in Luke 19:

Jesus entered Jericho and was passing through. A man was there by the name of Zacchaeus; he was a chief tax collector and was wealthy. He wanted to see who Jesus was, but because he was short he could not see over the crowd. So he ran ahead and climbed a sycamore-fig tree to see him, since Jesus was coming that way. When Jesus reached the spot, he looked up and said to him, "Zacchaeus, come down immediately. I must stay at your house today." So he came down at once and welcomed him gladly. All the people saw this and began to mutter, "He has gone to be the guest of a sinner." But Zacchaeus stood up and said to the Lord, "Look, Lord! Here and now I give half of my possessions to the poor, and if I have cheated anybody out of anything, I will pay back four times the amount." Jesus said to him, "Today salvation has come to this house, because this man, too, is a son of Abraham. For the Son of Man came to seek and to save the lost."

—Luke 19:1–10, niv

Therefore to him that knoweth to do good, and doeth it not, to him it is sin.

—James 4:17

Giving tithes and offerings is simply the right and Christian thing to do. Don't strive with your Maker over this issue.

Woe unto him that striveth with his Maker! Let the potsherd strive with the potsherds of the earth. Shall the clay say to him that fashioneth it, What makest thou? Or thy work, He hath no hands?

—Isaiah 45:9

Go to your pastor with all your questions on tithes and offerings if you are facing challenges in this area.

To obey is better than sacrifice.

—1 Samuel 15:22b

A lying tongue hateth those that are afflicted by it; and a flattering mouth worketh ruin.

—Proverbs 26:28

Bring the whole tithe into the storehouse, that there may be food in my house. Test me in this," says the LORD Almighty, "and see if I will not throw open the floodgates of heaven and pour out so much blessing that there will not be room enough to store it. I will prevent pests from devouring your crops, and the vines in your fields will not drop their fruit before it is ripe," says the LORD Almighty.

—MALACHI 3:10–11, NIV

Do not be deceived and deluded and misled; God will not allow Himself to be sneered at (scorned, disdained, or mocked by mere pretensions or professions, or by His precepts being set aside.) [He inevitably deludes himself who attempts to delude God.] For whatever a man sows, that and that only is what he will reap.

[GALATIANS 6:7, AMP]

Chapter 4
THE CURSE OF SEEDTIME AND HARVEST

While the earth remaineth, seedtime and harvest, and cold and heat, and summer and winter, and day and night shall not cease.
—GENESIS 8:22

MIKE MURDOCK ONCE said, "You are a walking warehouse of seeds...It is tragic beyond words if you fail to recognize your seeds."[1]

Whereas the above quote is in direct reference to positive seeds that benefit you, the opposite is also true. Negative seeds can also impact, haunt, and become a curse to you.

Harvests are always greater than the seed. When you plant a grain of corn, your harvest could be several kernels on each cob.

> Knowing that whatsoever good thing any man doeth, the same shall he receive of the Lord, whether he be bond or free.
> —EPHESIANS 6:8

The curse of harvesttime and seedtime is self-inflicted. You cannot sow corn and expect rice at harvesttime. The sowing and harvesttimes fall under different seasons, and sometimes the negative seeds that you sow may catch up with you at old age when you should be retired and enjoying life. It is very common and easy for people to forget the evil and negative seeds sown for sometimes the harvest may be in the distant future, even as a ripple effect on later generations.

The ministry of the apostle Paul was plagued with much suffering. Paul persecuted the church and made their lives miserable. By the zeal of his youth, he ignorantly sowed seeds of suffering and pain within the church of Jesus Christ. After his conversion, God told Ananias concerning Paul: "For I will shew him how great things he must suffer for my name's sake" (Acts 9:16).

Have you teamed up to defame anyone? Have you joined with

others to destroy somebody's handy work or ministry? Have you been an accomplice to anybody's downfall? Have you cursed anyone? Have you treated that which belongs to another man carelessly? Have you lied to get anybody in trouble? Have you robbed anyone? Have you desired evil on your neighbors? Have you been insubordinate to your leader? All these and more matter to God, for the law of seedtime and harvesttime is irrevocable.

> Great in counsel, and mighty in work: for thine eyes are open upon all the ways of the sons of men: to give everyone according to his ways, and according to the fruit of his doings.
> —JEREMIAH 32:19

Jesus said, "The scripture cannot be broken" (John 10:35b). You will reap what you sow; if you sow evil, you will reap evil.

Many young pastors in their zeal without knowledge have scattered somebody's church to build their own. Oh, how I pray that they will go back to make things right with their former pastor and with God. Don't allow pride to ruin your grace.

DAVID, URIAH, AND BATHSHEBA

David had an affair with Bathsheba, the wife of Uriah. When he found out that she had conceived by him, David came up with a plan to hide his sin, shame, and guilt by getting Uriah drunk and so the pregnancy might be attributed to him. When that failed, David quickly moved to "plan B." He invented the "letter bomb," which sent Uriah to the battlefront where he lost his life, indirect murder at the hands of David. This "sword" in the form of death was released upon David's household.

Read the entire story in 2 Samuel 11:1–27. The scriptures cannot be broken; you reap what you sow. See the terrible harvest David reaped in 2 Samuel 16:22: "So they spread Absalom a tent upon the top of the house: and Absalom went in unto his father's concubines in the sight of all Israel."

AHAB, JEZEBEL, AND NABOTH

King Ahab and his wife Jezebel conspired and killed Naboth for his vineyard. The story is recorded in 1 Kings 21. The seed of greed and envy is a terrible combination to sow; the harvest you reap can be very dangerous and deadly. Look at the terrible judgment pronounced on them through the prophet Elijah;

> Then the word of the LORD came to Elijah the Tishbite: "Go down to meet Ahab king of Israel, who rules in Samaria. He is now in Naboth's vineyard, where he has gone to take possession of it. Say to him, 'This is what the LORD says: Have you not murdered a man and seized his property?' Then say to him, 'This is what the LORD says: In the place where dogs licked up Naboth's blood, dogs will lick up your blood—yes, yours!'" Ahab said to Elijah, "So you have found me, my enemy!" "I have found you," he answered, "because you have sold yourself to do evil in the eyes of the LORD. He says, 'I am going to bring disaster on you. I will wipe out your descendants and cut off from Ahab every last male in Israel—slave or free. I will make your house like that of Jeroboam son of Nebat and that of Baasha son of Ahijah, because you have aroused my anger and have caused Israel to sin.'"
>
> —1 KINGS 21:17–22, NIV

Evil seeds sown will always produce a harvest of pain and sorrow. "Evil shall slay the wicked" (Ps. 34:21a).

Seedtime and harvesttime is an unchangeable law of God that governs the universe. No one can escape it. You reap what you sow.

> Every man shall kiss his lips that giveth a right answer. Prepare thy work without, and make it fit for thyself in the field; and afterwards build thine house. Be not a witness against thy neighbour without cause; and deceive not with thy lips.
>
> —PROVERBS 24:26–28

It's a good place to pause for prayer. The Holy Ghost came as your Helper and He is ready even now to help you only if you ask.

Heavenly Father, Your Word declares that You overlook our times of ignorance. I have in my ignorance sown many seeds to my hurt. I ask for Your forgiveness and mercy through the precious blood of Jesus Christ. Holy Spirit, help me to uproot every seed negatively planted so that I might escape every pending harvest. I repent from my sin and break the power of every self-imposed curse. I contact grace to sow good seeds from henceforth in Jesus' name!

For vexation and rage kill the foolish man; jeal-
ousy and indignation slay the simple.
[JOB 5:2, AMP]

Do not be quick in spirit to be angry or vexed, for anger
and vexation lodge in the bosom of fools.
[ECCLESIASTES 7:9, AMP]

Chapter 5
THE CURSE OF ANGER, RESENTMENT, AND BITTERNESS

ANGER, RESENTMENT, AND bitterness are very closely related and work together to create havoc, horrible destruction, pain, and death. Their victims are captives subject to do their bidding until they are consumed and totally destroyed.

The first mention of this subject is recorded of the first family God created. Shortly after the fall of man, Adam and Eve began to raise their family beginning with two brothers. The same enemy that deceived them now set his eyes on the brothers. Satan planted an evil seed of anger, bitterness, and resentment in the heart of Cain. According to John the Beloved, Cain belonged to the evil one: "Not as Cain, who was of that wicked one, and slew his brother. And wherefore slew he him? Because his own works were evil, and his brother's righteous" (1 John 3:12).

Cain enticed his brother away from home and by reason of the seed within him; he killed Abel in cold blood.

> And in the process of time it came to pass that Cain brought an offering of the fruit of the ground to the Lord. Abel also brought of the firstborn of his flock and of their fat. And the Lord respected Abel and his offering, but He did not respect Cain and his offering. And Cain was very angry, and his countenance fell. So the Lord said to Cain, "Why are you angry? And why has your countenance fallen? If you do well, will you not be accepted? And if you do not do well, sin lies at the door. And its desire is for you, but you should rule over it."
> —Genesis 4:3–7, nkjv

Your season of blessing will come. But are you happy for others when they make it in their particular season and you don't? How about when others are favored or preferred or chosen over you? Are you resentful, secretly bitter, angry, and/or envious? Do you join others to gossip about them? In your heart do you desire their downfall?

These and many other questions can help you check yourself and bring your Christian life back into alignment with the Word of God and the will of God for your life. Bitterness, anger, and resentment are the curse of the vagabond—a wanderer with no permanent address who can't seem to hold on to anything, be it a job, business, or relationship, and the list goes on. Read the judgment of Cain from the lips of God Himself:

> And now art thou cursed from the earth, which hath opened her mouth to receive thy brother's blood from thy hand; When thou tillest the ground, it shall not henceforth yield unto thee her strength; a fugitive and a vagabond shalt thou be in the earth.
> —GENESIS 4:11–12

Envy graduates and matures into anger, and anger matures into bitterness. Together they bring you under the curse of the vagabond.

Look at this very intriguing scripture:

> Follow peace with all men, and holiness, without which no man shall see the Lord: Looking diligently lest any man fail of the grace of God; lest any root of bitterness springing up trouble you, and thereby many be defiled.
> —HEBREWS 12:14–15

The root of bitterness can trouble you and cause you to lose your salvation. It will cause the heavens above you to become brass and iron. Hear me, child of God; you cannot use a strong iron face to force God to bless you when you walk in resentment, anger, and bitterness. Contact grace from God to escape this "plague."

- It is a devourer.
- It is a killer.
- It is a destroyer.
- It will ensnare and lock you into a grave.

Get rid of your anger now before it gets rid of you! Don't be like the foolish servant who was incarcerated until he paid all that he owed:

"And his lord was wroth, and delivered him to the tormentors, till he should pay all that was due unto him" (Matt. 18:34).

REVENGE

Anger provokes revenge. Revenge is a product of anger, unforgiveness, and bitterness. It can also operate against you under the curse of seedtime, harvesttime, and the shedding innocent blood. Oftentimes when people feel violated in any area of their lives, they nurse the hurt for years in their heart. The root of this bitterness festers long enough to become a stronghold clouding their judgment. Some end up committing suicide while others plan retaliation through violence. Some leave suicidal notes justifying their violent rampage.

In recent times, gun violence has been on the increase; this is all connected to revenge. We've seen it on the news. No neighborhood is exempt. Nations are rising against each other in revenge. In fact, it is one of many signs of the end time and Satan is the mastermind behind it all. Our government is doing everything to curb the violence but they can only do so much, because it is spiritual and it is a curse. While I hope this book keeps the discussion on gun violence alive, my prayer is for the church to unit in prayer to deal with the root cause and arrest the behind-the-scenes force. This curse has already claimed too many lives and the blood of each victim is crying out from the earth. Marching and demonstrating with signs may be okay and play their role in hope of solving the problem; but that can't detect or arrest demons. Prayer on our knees in the secret place does. We must all engage to do our part both government and the church.

The Bible is full of many stories of revenge and the consequences. Absalom was the handsome prince of Israel. He had a bright future and loved by his people—they bowed before him. But Absalom was a rebel. After he killed his brother Amnon in revenge for the rape of their sister, he stayed in exile for a season but then returned to fight his father, King David, for not addressing the dysfunction in the family. He teamed up with Ahitophel, David's chief counselor, who was also bitter towards David in the incident of Beersheba, his granddaughter, and Uriah the Hittite, his son-in-law. The shameful act of revenge by the prince started a civil war that claimed over twenty thousand casualties. Both Absalom and Ahitophel died horrible deaths. The corpse

of the young prince was dumped into a large pit and stones rolled over
it in dishonor. This story is recorded in 2 Samuel 13–19.

How terrible is the curse of revenge; nobody wins!

We must not take matters into our own hands by enforcing vengeance to vindicate ourselves. Vengeance belongs to God. "Dearly
beloved, avenge not yourselves, but rather give place unto wrath: for
it is written, Vengeance is mine; I will repay, saith the Lord" (Rom.
12:19).

Oftentimes people justify anger by saying, "You don't know what
they did to me; you are not in my shoes." Anger will hinder your
prayers and prevent your increase.

> Therefore, if you are offering your gift at the altar and there
> remember that your brother or sister has something against you,
> leave your gift there in front of the altar. First go and be rec-
> onciled to them; then come and offer your gift. Settle matters
> quickly with your adversary who is taking you to court. Do it
> while you are still together on the way, or your adversary may
> hand you over to the judge, and the judge may hand you over to
> the officer, and you may be thrown into prison.
>
> —MATTHEW 5:23–25, NIV

Anger will blind and block your perception; it will cloud and distort
your judgment and keep you in the dark. "He that saith he is in the
light, and hateth his brother, is in darkness even until now" (1 John
2:9).

Unchecked anger will eventually rob you of your promised land.
Moses is the fourth generation in the bloodline of Levi. His anger could
be traced to his great-grandparent Levi who was cursed by the patriarch Jacob several generations before Moses was born: "Cursed be their
anger, for it was fierce; and their wrath, for it was cruel: I will divide
them in Jacob, and scatter them in Israel" (Gen. 49:7).

After the great victory over Pharaoh and all the gods of Egypt,
Moses led the exodus of Israel out of captivity through the Red Sea.
He battled giants, and suffered the insubordination of his own people.
Moses, the humble great prophet, deliverer, and leader of God's
people, came so close to accomplishing his mission—to enter the
Promised Land; but anger robbed him at the point of entry. After all

his accomplishments in ministry, it came down to what is recorded in the Book of Numbers.

> And the LORD spake unto Moses and Aaron, Because ye believed me not, to sanctify me in the eyes of the children of Israel, therefore ye shall not bring this congregation into the land which I have given them.
>
> —NUMBERS 20:12

The root cause for this scripture can be summed up in one word—*anger*. At age forty, as a prince in Egypt, Moses lost his temper and killed an Egyptian soldier and hid the body in the sand (see Exodus 2:11–14).

There are people in spiritual prison living in fear because of things they are hiding in the sand as a result of uncontrolled anger. But it's time to bring it out, stop running and hiding from your mess and dirty laundry, and run to God to be forgiven and delivered.

In his zeal and anger, Moses broke the original tablets upon which God wrote the Ten Commandments with His finger. When Moses approached the camp and saw the golden calf and dancing going on in honor of an idol god, his anger burned hot within him, causing him to lose his temper. He threw the tablets out of his hands, breaking them to pieces at the foot of the mountain. Then he took the golden calf and burned it in the fire, ground it into powder, scattered it into the water, and made the Israelites drink it (Exod. 32:19–20). He said to Aaron,

> "What did these people do to you, that you led them into such great sin?" "Do not be angry, my lord," Aaron answered. "You know how prone these people are to evil. They said to me, 'Make us gods who will go before us. As for this fellow Moses who brought us up out of Egypt, we don't know what has happened to him.' So I told them, 'Whoever has any gold jewelry, take it off.' Then they gave me the gold, and I threw it into the fire, and out came this calf!" Moses saw that the people were running wild and that Aaron had let them get out of control and so become a laughingstock to their enemies. So he stood at the entrance to the camp and said, "Whoever is for the LORD, come to me." And all the Levites rallied to him. Then he said to them, "This is what the LORD, the God of Israel, says: 'Each man strap a sword to his side. Go back and

forth through the camp from one end to the other, each killing his brother and friend and neighbor.'" The Levites did as Moses commanded, and that day about three thousand of the people died. Then Moses said, "You have been set apart to the LORD today, for you were against your own sons and brothers, and he has blessed you this day." The next day Moses said to the people, "You have committed a great sin. But now I will go up to the LORD; perhaps I can make atonement for your sin." So Moses went back to the LORD and said, "Oh, what a great sin these people have committed! They have made themselves gods of gold. But now, please forgive their sin but if not, then blot me out of the book you have written." The LORD replied to Moses, "Whoever has sinned against me I will blot out of my book. Now go, lead the people to the place I spoke of, and my angel will go before you. However, when the time comes for me to punish, I will punish them for their sin." And the LORD struck the people with a plague because of what they did with the calf Aaron had made.

—EXODUS 32:21–35, NIV

It tells in Exodus 32:20 how, in his anger, Moses made the children of Israel drink polluted water. Paul tells us, "Be ye angry, and sin not: let not the sun go down upon your wrath" (Eph. 4:26).

In Numbers 20:10–12 we read where God instructed Moses to speak to the rock, which was a symbol of Christ, to produce water for the people. He lost his cool and struck the rock. His anger and disobedience dishonored God, and it cost him the Promised Land. God is a rewarder and faithful to His Word (Heb. 11:6), He honored Moses and fulfilled His promise to him when He brought Moses and Elijah to stand with Jesus on the Mount of Transfiguration (see Luke 9:27–36.)

Oh, the mercies of God and His great wisdom, how unsearchable (Rom. 11:33)!

SOULISH PRAYERS

Soulish prayer is simply witchcraft in the church. It causes havoc and confusion, and its roots can be traced directly to Satan, who is the author of confusion. A Christian praying soulish prayers is simply using his God-given authority to release demonic activities in the church. Jesus delegated to us the authority to bind and loose, and we must not abuse this awesome grace.

> And I will give unto thee the keys of the kingdom of heaven: and whatsoever thou shalt bind on earth shall be bound in heaven: and whatsoever thou shalt loose on earth shall be loosed in heaven.
>
> —MATTHEW 16:19

Some Christians have brought curses upon themselves by engaging in soulish prayers. Such prayers undermine the will of God and His original intent, plan, and purpose for an individual's life. It is motivated by self-righteousness, anger, envy, resentment, criticism, and other forms of fleshly desires. These prayers are often for self-gratification and can be very condemnatory, intimidating, harassing, manipulative, accusatory, and dominating. Superimposing your desire through prayer to manipulate the destiny of others is soulish prayer. King Solomon revealed that this kind of prayer is an abomination unto God: "He that turneth away his ear from hearing the law, even his prayer shall be abomination" (Prov. 28:9).

Soulish prayer can also be defined as prayer outside the will of God. In fact, it is coming into agreement with Satan's desires. God does not and will not answer or honor such prayers. Apostle James wrote, "Ye ask, and receive not, because ye ask amiss, that ye may consume it upon your lusts" (James 4:3).

Soulish prayers open the door for demons and fallen angels to mess with you, because Satan is the one who eventually answers such prayers. God has not called us to manipulate and accuse each other. Manipulation is witchcraft, and the Book of Revelation clearly points Satan out as the accuser of the brethren.

> And I heard a loud voice saying in heaven, Now is come salvation, and strength, and the kingdom of our God, and the power of his Christ: for the accuser of our brethren is cast down, which accused them before our God day and night.
>
> —REVELATION 12:10

In one of his numerous teachings on prayer, the Archbishop Duncan Williams said, "You are either an intercessor or accuser of the brethren."[1]

May you never be counted among the accusers! The price for this kind of practice can be very detrimental. According to James 3:15, it is simply demonic. Sincere and honest prayers must be according to the will of the Holy Spirit and directed to our heavenly Father.

> Likewise the Spirit also helpeth our infirmities: for we know not what we should pray for as we ought: but the Spirit itself maketh intercession for us with groanings which cannot be uttered. And he that searcheth the hearts knoweth what is the mind of the Spirit, because he maketh intercession for the saints according to the will of God.
>
> —Romans 8:26–27

The church has absolute power over the entire demonic kingdom: "Behold, I give unto you power to tread on serpents and scorpions, and over all the power of the enemy: and nothing shall by any means hurt you" (Luke 10:19).

Power came from heaven to transform the New Testament church into world changers and community transformers on the day of Pentecost. This authority must be properly channeled through the rules of engagement. When engaging in spiritual warfare prayer, it should be directed at the enemy and his works, not at a believer. Let us honor each other, and ultimately the King, by praying down His blessings to bless humanity. It is the Christian thing to do according to the teachings of Jesus, who Himself is our ultimate example: "But I say unto you, Love your enemies, bless them that curse you, do good to them that hate you, and pray for them which despitefully use you, and persecute you" (Matt. 5:44).

A Christian who engages in soulish prayers, causing havoc and confusion in the church, gives an occasion to the enemies of God to triumph and reproaches the name of the Lord. The question to consider, however, is whether you will be happy being on the receiving end of such careless destructive soulish prayers. As believers we must practice what we preach and teach. Peter admonished us in his Epistle not to repay anyone evil for evil. This practice is below our dignity and should not be tolerated or even mentioned among us as followers of Christ. "Not rendering evil for evil, or railing for railing: but contrariwise blessing; knowing that ye are thereunto called, that ye should inherit a blessing" (1 Pet. 3:9).

This is the way of the kingdom of God and the example Jesus left for us to follow.

How to Break the Curse

One of the most intriguing statements I ever heard on the subject of unforgiveness was on TBN by Dr. Dwight Thompson. He said,

> When you forgive and release and let somebody else go, while it does not make them right, it will make you free. When you hold an offense it is like drinking poison and expecting somebody else to die. If you want to be free, forgive them and let them go.[2]

Unforgiveness is spiritual poison that slowly affects every part of your being form inside out.

Forgiveness is the best antidote in breaking the curse. You must apply the blood of Jesus and pray for all those who offended you and provoked you to the point of anger and bitterness. Pray for grace and against envy and stay in the mirror of the Word of God.

As a protégé of the Archbishop Duncan Williams, I watched him go through betrayals time and again. How he handled his pain; the tremendous effort he made through the grace of God upon his life to forgive and restore his sons and daughters in ministry who turned against him and many others who took undue advantage of doors he opened for them; and his prayers and mentorship greatly prepared me for my hour of pain. It's a lifelong lesson that I do not take for granted nor will I ever forget it. It is also one of the reasons why I personally encourage ministers, especially younger ones coming into ministry, to have a mentor they can look up to, respect, and submit to.

As a minister of the gospel, I reached out and helped many selflessly. The very people I loved and helped the most were those the enemy used to try to destroy my ministry. The experience was very painful; I thought my world will cave in on me. Many doors were shut in my face. It felt like God had forsaken me. The heavens seemed closed to me for that season, partly because I didn't let go quick enough. The conspiracy of lies and manipulation was so strong. I have watched this happen to many people, including my father in the Lord, the

Archbishop Duncan Williams. I didn't know how painful this could be until it happened to me. I actually thought I was immune and exempt from this kind of attack. My family came under strong attack; nobody wanted to identify with me. It was not easy; it almost crippled me completely. But when I let go, my healing began and the heavens opened up to me and I was restored and my ministry.

HELPFUL SCRIPTURES

Wherefore, my beloved brethren, let every man be swift to hear, slow to speak, slow to wrath: For the wrath of man worketh not the righteousness of God. Wherefore lay apart all filthiness and superfluity of naughtiness, and receive with meekness the engrafted word, which is able to save your souls.

—JAMES 1:19–21

Be ye angry, and sin not: let not the sun go down upon your wrath.

—EPHESIANS 4:26

He that is soon angry dealeth foolishly: and a man of wicked devices is hated.

—PROVERBS 14:17

Make no friendship with an angry man; and with a furious man thou shalt not go.

—PROVERBS 22:24

A wrathful man stirreth up strife: but he that is slow to anger appeaseth strife.

—PROVERBS 15:18

He that is slow to wrath is of great understanding: but he that is hasty of spirit exalteth folly.

—PROVERBS 14:29

He that is slow to anger is better than the mighty; and he that ruleth his spirit than he that taketh a city.

—PROVERBS 16:32

An angry man stirreth up strife, and a furious man aboundeth in transgression.

—PROVERBS 29:22

Soft answer turneth away wrath: but grievous words stir up anger.

—PROVERBS 15:1

Thou shalt not hate thy brother in thine heart: thou shalt in any wise rebuke thy neighbour, and not suffer sin upon him. Thou shalt not avenge, nor bear any grudge against the children of thy people, but thou shalt love thy neighbour as thyself: I am the LORD.

—LEVITICUS 19:17–18

But now ye also put off all these; anger, wrath, malice, blasphemy, filthy communication out of your mouth.

—COLOSSIANS 3:8

Be not hasty in thy spirit to be angry: for anger resteth in the bosom of fools.

—ECCLESIASTES 7:9

For wrath killeth the foolish man, and envy slayeth the silly one.

—JOB 5:2

ANGER QUOTES

- Ambrose Bierce: "Speak when you are angry and you will make the best speech you will ever regret."[3]

- Anonymous: "Anger is a condition in which the tongue works faster than the mind."[4]

- Virgil Aeneid: "Anger supplies arms."[5]

- Maya Angelou: "Bitterness is like cancer. It eats upon the host. But anger is like fire. It burns it all clean."[6]

- Daniel Webster: "Keep cool; anger is not an argument."[7]

- Bible: "Anger resteth in the bosom of fools" (Eccles. 7:9b).

- John Webster: "There is not in a nature, a thing that makes man so deformed, so beastly, as doth intemperate anger."[8]

Now pray this prayer:

Lord, deliver me from the curse of anger and bitterness. I totally renounce them and break their power over my life. Holy Spirit, You are the breaker. Break the curse and deliver me from the stronghold of anger, resentment, and bitterness. Now fill me with joy and peace and give me the grace to be happy for others, knowing very well that my time to shine will come, in Jesus' name!

Regard (treat with honor, due obedience, and courtesy) your father and mother, that your days may be long in the land the Lord your God gives you.
[Exodus 20:12, AMP]

Whoever curses his father or his mother, his lamp shall be put out in complete darkness.
[Proverbs 20:20, AMP]

Chapter 6

THE CURSE OF AUTHORITY FIGURES

I N THIS CHAPTER, we will consider how parental curses and those of spiritual figures affect an individual.

DISHONOR TO PARENTS

God commanded the children of Israel to honor their parents because it is the honorable thing to do and carries with it the promise of long life on earth. "Honour thy father and thy mother: that thy days may be long upon the land which the LORD thy God giveth thee" (Exod. 20:12).

God reaffirmed it through the apostle Paul for emphasis to the New Testament church, comprising of both Jews and Gentiles, so that no one would have an excuse for exemption:

> Children, obey your parents in the Lord: for this is right. "Honor your father and mother"—which is the first commandment with a promise—"so that it may go well with you and that you may enjoy long life on the earth."
> —EPHESIANS 6:1–3

This is not a suggestion or just another good idea; it was and still is and will remain a command by God with a reward. The direct opposite is to dishonor your parents and be taken out in the prime of your life. It is a matter of choice.

Ephesians 6:13: has a twofold meaning:

1. "Obey your parents in the Lord" refers to spiritual parents.

2. "Honor you father and mother" is a direct reference to your natural parents who gave birth to you.

Let's separate these into two categories for further study, beginning with the latter.

HONORING YOUR NATURAL PARENTS

Dishonoring your natural parents carries dire consequences; yet conversely, when you honor them, you reap tremendous blessings. To dishonor a parent is to dishonor God. God made no mistake when He chose to bring you into this world through your parents. They fit in God's plan for your destiny and carry "parental" authority. Their words spoken over you will have direct impact on you, whether positively or negatively.

Many children have provoked their parents to anger; and in their anger, they have released cursing words, some knowingly and others ignorantly. In each case, the children remain under the curse until it is broken. Remember, "Death and life are in the power of the tongue" (Prov. 18:21).

Examples of damaging words:

1. I regret having you as my child.

2. You are good for nothing.

3. You will never amount to anything.

Such cursing words may haunt the children throughout their lives and exact upon them great pain and frustration. Many successful children have dishonored their parents by abandoning them in senior homes. Their success and schedules have made them too busy to be bothered with the old and ailing parent. Senior homes maybe a blessing, but some children have used them to get rid of their parents so they can go on with their lives. When was the last time you took time to celebrate and appreciate your parents?

Following are a few biblical examples of children who dishonored parents and reaped the consequences of their actions.

Ham dishonored Noah

> And Noah began to be a husbandman, and he planted a vineyard: And he drank of the wine, and was drunken; and he was

uncovered within his tent. And Ham, the father of Canaan, saw
the nakedness of his father, and told his two brethren without.

—GENESIS 9:20–22

Look at the consequences:

And Noah awoke from his wine, and knew what his younger son
had done unto him. And he said, Cursed be Canaan; a servant of
servants shall he be unto his brethren.

—GENESIS 9:24–25

The Canaanites were among the nations that God told Israel to dispossess when they left Egypt. Why would God honor the curse words
of the drunken Noah? Proverbs 20:20 declares: "Whoso curseth his
father or his mother, his lamp shall be put out in obscure darkness."

Consider Psalm 68:6: "God setteth the solitary in families: he bringeth
out those which are bound with chains: but the rebellious dwell in a dry
land." Dishonor to parents will bring you into a dry land. A dry land is
a place of unnecessary toil, struggle, and frustration. Many believers are
in a dry land because of dishonor to parents.

Absalom dishonors David

*Absalom and Solomon had the same father. Solomon honored his
father and sat on the throne as the next king after David. Absalom dishonored his father and hanged from a tree to his death.*

And Absalom met the servants of David. And Absalom rode
upon a mule, and the mule went under the thick boughs of a
great oak, and his head caught hold of the oak, and he was taken
up between the heaven and the earth; and the mule that was
under him went away.

—2 SAMUEL 18:9

*Poor Absalom; he had the looks and he was the people's choice, but
God rejected him. The curse of dishonor locked him into an early grave.
Please don't be the next victim.*

Jesus emphasized honoring parents during His brief encounter with
the rich young ruler:

And behold, there came a man up to Him, saying, Teacher, what excellent and perfectly and essentially good deed must I do to possess eternal life? And He said to him, Why do you ask me about the perfectly and essentially good? There is only One who is good [perfectly and essentially]—God. If you would enter into the Life, you must continually keep the commandments. He said to Him, What sort of commandments? [Or, which ones?] And Jesus answered, You shall not kill, You shall not commit adultery, You shall not steal, You shall not bear false witness, Honor your father and your mother, and, You shall love your neighbor as [you do] yourself.

—MATTHEW 19:16–19, AMP

Honoring parents was so important to Jesus that to honor His mother, He even put death on hold while on the cross.

Now there stood by the cross of Jesus his mother, and his mother's sister, Mary the wife of Cleophas, and Mary Magdalene. When Jesus therefore saw his mother, and the disciple standing by, whom he loved, he saith unto his mother, Woman, behold thy son! Then saith he to the disciple, Behold thy mother! And from that hour that disciple took her unto his own home.

—JOHN 19:25–27

If you have dishonored your parents in any way, this might be a good time to call them and get it right with them. The curse is broken the moment you come into divine compliance with them and the Word of God. If they have already gone to be with the Lord, may grace and mercy restore you, in the name of Jesus the Christ.

DISHONORING SPIRITUAL PARENTS

This group includes the ministers that God has set in a place of authority over you—your pastor, bishop, prophet, and/or spiritual mentor. The apostle Paul pointed out the fact that there are spiritual fathers.

For though ye have ten thousand instructors in Christ, yet have ye not many fathers: for in Christ Jesus I have begotten you through the gospel. Wherefore I beseech you, be ye followers of me.

—1 CORINTHIANS 4:15–16

God is very protective of the shepherds He has placed over you: "He suffered no man to do them wrong: yea, he reproved kings for their sakes; Saying, Touch not mine anointed, and do my prophets no harm" (Ps. 105:14–15).

It is suicidal to dishonor a spiritual authority or touch God's anointed. The curses you incur are very detrimental.

Many Christians have touched or dishonored spiritual figures in their lives. Because they did not fall and die immediately, they have taken this long-suffering of God to be permission and "license to kill." Therefore, they continue in this very dangerous activity.

Dissension of Aaron and Miriam

> And Miriam and Aaron spake against Moses because of the Ethiopian woman whom he had married: for he had married an Ethiopian woman. And they said, Hath the LORD indeed spoken only by Moses? hath he not spoken also by us? And the LORD heard it. (Now the man Moses was very meek, above all the men which were upon the face of the earth.) And the LORD spake suddenly unto Moses, and unto Aaron, and unto Miriam, Come out ye three unto the tabernacle of the congregation. And they three came out. And the LORD came down in the pillar of the cloud, and stood in the door of the tabernacle, and called Aaron and Miriam: and they both came forth. And he said, Hear now my words: If there be a prophet among you, I the LORD will make myself known unto him in a vision, and will speak unto him in a dream. My servant Moses is not so, who is faithful in all mine house. With him will I speak mouth to mouth, even apparently, and not in dark speeches; and the similitude of the LORD shall he behold: wherefore then were ye not afraid to speak against my servant Moses? And the anger of the LORD was kindled against them; and he departed. And the cloud departed from off the tabernacle; and, behold, Miriam became leprous, white as snow: and Aaron looked upon Miriam, and, behold, she was leprous. And Aaron said unto Moses, Alas, my lord, I beseech thee, lay not the sin upon us, wherein we have done foolishly, and wherein we have sinned. Let her not be as one dead, of whom the flesh is half consumed when he cometh out of his mother's womb. And Moses cried unto the LORD, saying, Heal her now, O God, I beseech thee. And the LORD said unto Moses, If her father had but spit in her face, should she not be ashamed seven days?

let her be shut out from the camp seven days, and after that let her be received in again. And Miriam was shut out from the camp seven days: and the people journeyed not till Miriam was brought in again. And afterward the people removed from Hazeroth, and pitched in the wilderness of Paran.

—Numbers 12:1–16

Aaron and Miriam opposed Moses and provoked God to come down to the defense of His anointed. By the time the cloud lifted, the judgment was clear; Miriam was struck with leprosy and it took the intercession of Moses to save her. It is ironic that the thing about which they opposed Moses, God did not address. Why? Because everyone must learn to allow God to deal with His servants and not take matters into their own hands.

Have you opposed your leader and God's chosen vessel either publicly or privately, even if it happened in your heart where no one saw it or in the comfort of your home? The best remedy to stop the effect of this curse and break its power over your life and bloodline is to sincerely repent in your heart and go before your leader and ask them to pray for you. Every time you are tempted to dishonor spiritual authority, remember:

For the earth which drinketh in the rain that cometh oft upon it, and bringeth forth herbs meet for them by whom it is dressed, receiveth blessing from God: But that which beareth thorns and briers is rejected, and is nigh unto cursing; whose end is to be burned.

—Hebrews 6:7–8

It's only a matter of time before it catches up with you. It is better to watch a news channel and criticize them than to watch Christian television and be tempted to accuse a servant of God. May you never again fall into the trap of dishonor. Bishop Michael Pitts once said, "The spirit of dishonor is like bringing a wild tiger home thinking you can tame it."[1]

PARENTAL ADMONISHMENT

And, ye fathers, provoke not your children to wrath: but bring them up in the nurture and admonition of the Lord.

—EPHESIANS 6:4

Wives, submit yourselves unto your own husbands, as it is fit in the Lord. Husbands, love your wives, and be not bitter against them. Children, obey your parents in all things: for this is well pleasing unto the Lord. Fathers, provoke not your children to anger, lest they be discouraged.

—COLOSSIANS 3:18–21

Please, parents, it is our godly duty to raise up our children in the fear of the Lord. Imposing the culture of when you were young on them may not help, since they are living and growing in a different generation. There has to be a balance of understanding of the times. We must maintain biblical principles in our homes through family prayer times and Bible study. There has to be time set apart to discuss family matters and challenges of the times.

Lo, children are an heritage of the LORD: and the fruit of the womb is his reward. As arrows are in the hand of a mighty man; so are children of the youth. Happy is the man that hath his quiver full of them: they shall not be ashamed, but they shall speak with the enemies in the gate.

—PSALM 127:3–5

You are a steward over God's heritage. Be an example for them not only in words but also in deed. You should be their number one role model. God appointed you into that office. This is why you are the parent and not the person they watch on television.

Parental authority should be used wisely under the guidance of the Scriptures and the leading of the Holy Spirit. Abuse of this power can open the door to a chain reaction of disregard, disrespect, and a host of other things that could be detrimental to the parent-child relationship.

May the grace of God that keeps families together come upon your household. May the Spirit of God brood over you and your children, sustain, keep, and preserve you, in Jesus' name.

He who goes about as a talebearer reveals secrets; there-
fore associate not with him who talks too freely.
[PROVERBS 20:19, AMP]

You shall not go up and down as a dispenser of gossip and scandal
among your people, nor shall you [secure yourself by false testimony
or by silence and] endanger the life of your neighbor. I am the Lord.
[LEVITICUS 19:16, AMP]

Chapter 7
THE CURSE OF GOSSIP

EVIL COMMUNICATION

COMMON PRACTICE OF many believers is casually engaging in gossip.

Gossip is cancerous, it is poisonous and deadly. Whether you know it or not gossip is character assassination.

It defames its victims and subjects them to shame, reproach, devastation and ruin. It leaves many wounded and others slain in its destructive path. When you become the subject of gossip, it will require the grace of God to sustain you. It is easy to survive gossip when it's coming from the secular world, because it is expected; but when it comes from fellow believers, the pain is severe.

David said,

> My enemies say of me in malice, "When will he die and his name perish?" When one of them comes to see me, he speaks falsely, while his heart gathers slander; then he goes out and spreads it around. All my enemies whisper together against me; they imagine the worst for me, saying, "A vile disease has afflicted him; he will never get up from the place where he lies." Even my close friend, someone I trusted, one who shared my bread, has turned against me.
>
> —PSALM 41:5–9, NIV

David could handle the ungodly when they gossiped; but how do you deal with it when it's coming from brethren. Consider this statement by Samson: "And they said unto him, We are come down to bind thee, that we may deliver thee into the hand of the Philistines. And Samson said unto them, Swear unto me, that ye will not fall upon me yourselves" (Judg. 15:12). He made them promise that they themselves will not fall on him. In other words, "I know how to deal with the enemy; but how do I handle you the brethren?"

Let's look at two dictionary definitions of *gossip*:

[1] One who runs house to house, tattling and telling news; an idle tattler. [2] The tattle of a gossip; groundless rumor. [3] To prate; to chat; to talk much. [4] To run about and tattle; to tell idle tales.[1]

[1] A report (often malicious) about the behavior of other people. [2] A person given to gossiping and divulging personal information about others. [3] Wag ones tongue; speak about others and reveal secrets or intimacies. [4] Talk socially without exchanging too much information.[2]

In his 2010 article online on the subject "Avoiding the Dangers of Gossip," Michael Wheeler said,

If what you are saying does not edify, lift up, or unify, it is gossip. And it does not matter if you started it or if you spread it, the damage is the same, the result is the same. The result is someone being hurt and ultimately loss of respect for all parties affected. There are typically three things that fan the destructive flames of gossip. The first being a self-righteous individual; be it a leader or subordinate. The self-righteous leader seeks to divide and tear others down, creating a wedge between relationships. They consistently see themselves as right and others as wrong. They claim to have integrity but their speech says otherwise. The second is loose lips. There is a saying in the Navy that all sailors past and present understand to be the golden rule while out to sea. It is "Loose Lips sink ships!" simply stated it means that unguarded speech may give useful information, helping the enemy to sink your ship. This is almost always the case when dealing with leaderships. Your words can come back to sink your ship! The third is receptive ear for gossip; letting it proceed without consequence is beckoning anger, discord, and dissolving any bonds of loyalty.[3]

Your boat sinking or staying afloat is in the power of your choice. Words carry the potency of causing catastrophic damage. Gossip can poison your environment, but grace is made available *now* to over-turn the captivity and put the enemy to shame.

Gossip in the Bible

The Bible puts it simply: "A gossip betrays a confidence, but a trust-worthy person keeps a secret" (Prov. 11:13, NIV). Many fine and good believers have been trapped into the snare of gossip. Oftentimes when people are offended, gossip becomes easier. Ignorantly they feed Satan's ultimate goal, which is "to steal, and to kill, and to destroy" (John 10:10a).

Satan, the source

In the Book of Revelation, we read the Bible account of the war that ultimately dismissed Satan from heaven.

> And there was war in heaven: Michael and his angels fought against the dragon; and the dragon fought and his angels, And prevailed not; neither was their place found any more in heaven. And the great dragon was cast out, that old serpent, called the Devil, and Satan, which deceiveth the whole world: he was cast out into the earth, and his angels were cast out with him.
> —REVELATION 12:7–9

The angels that followed Satan were not forced by weapons; it was through the deceptive tongue of gossip. The cataclysmic event that derailed Adam in the Garden of Eden, causing him to disobey God, started with gossip. Satan did not carry one single demon or weapon with him into the garden.

Read the encounter:

> Now the serpent was more crafty than any of the wild animals the LORD God had made. He said to the woman, "Did God really say, 'You must not eat from any tree in the garden'?" The woman said to the serpent, "We may eat fruit from the trees in the garden, but God did say, 'You must not eat fruit from the tree that is in the middle of the garden, and you must not touch it, or you will die.' "You will not certainly die," the serpent said to the woman. "For God knows that when you eat from it your

eyes will be opened, and you will be like God, knowing good
and evil."

—GENESIS 3:1–5, NIV

In verse 1 he started gossip: "Did God really say…?" Jesus said about
the devil, "There is no truth in him. When he speaketh a lie, he speaketh
of his own: for he is a liar, and the father of it" (John 8:44b).

Satan started a gossip of lies and Eve bought into it. In nearly six thousand years, he has never gone off duty; he is always on assignment using
innocent victims to spread vicious lies through gossip. He has destroyed
lives, families, marriages, ministries, nations, relationships, and businesses by pitting good people against each other, brother against brother,
sister against sister, neighbor against neighbor.

Verses 3 and 4 of Genesis 3 state: "But of the fruit of the tree which
is in the midst of the garden, God hath said, Ye shall not eat of it,
neither shall ye touch it, lest ye die. And the serpent said unto the
woman, Ye shall not surely die." He engaged Eve in gossip about the
integrity of God. He (Satan) questioned God's motive about the tree
of knowledge of good and evil.

> And out of the ground made the LORD God to grow every tree
> that is pleasant to the sight, and good for food; the tree of life
> also in the midst of the garden, and the tree of knowledge of
> good and evil.
>
> —GENESIS 2:9

The effect of Eve talking to the snake is the fall and a curse that has
affected the entire human race.

Gossip destroys

*Gossip is cancerous and poisonous; it should not be entertained on
any level or in any form or shape.*

> Without wood a fire goes out; without a gossip a quarrel dies
> down. As charcoal is to embers and as wood is to fire, so is a
> quarrelsome person for kindling strife. The words of a gossip are
> like choice morsels; they go down to the inmost parts.
>
> —PROVERBS 26:20–22, NIV

Both the talebearer and tale receiver are agents of strife, equally guilty. Don't entertain a gossiper and be an accomplice to their evil plot.

> Blessed is the man that walketh not in the counsel of the ungodly, nor standeth in the way of sinners, nor sitteth in the seat of the scornful.
> —PSALM 1:1

Gossip is contagious; please don't entertain gossipers.

> He that goeth about as a talebearer revealeth secrets: therefore meddle not with him that flattereth with his lips.
> —PROVERBS 20:19

God warned Israel in Leviticus 19:16: "Thou shalt not go up and down as a talebearer among thy people: neither shalt thou stand against the blood of thy neighbour; I am the LORD."

David was not only a king, he was also a prophet. He revealed that gossipers may not dwell in the presence of the Lord.

> LORD, who may dwell in your sacred tent? Who may live on your holy mountain? The one whose walk is blameless, who does what is righteous, who speaks the truth from their heart; whose tongue utters no slander, who does no wrong to a neighbor, and casts no slur on others.
> —PSALM 15:1–3, NIV

Why would a loving God forbid or banish anyone from His presence? Because gossip is an abomination to Him and He hates it.

> There are six things the LORD hates, seven that are detestable to him: haughty eyes, a lying tongue, hands that shed innocent blood, a heart that devises wicked schemes, feet that are quick to rush into evil, a false witness who pours out lies and a person who stirs up conflict in the community.
> —PROVERBS 6:16–19, NIV

I mentioned earlier that gossip kills. It has left many wounded and others slain. It has destroyed and divided churches. It has also caused many to walk away from the faith. Consider this warning from Jesus:

Jesus said to his disciples: "Things that cause people to stumble are bound to come, but woe to anyone through whom they come. It would be better for them to be thrown into the sea with a millstone tied around their neck than to cause one of these little ones to stumble.

—Luke 17:1–2, niv

Listen to me, child of God; gossip is a destroyer!

Daniel

In the days of Daniel, the governors and princes became envious and jealous of him. Through gossip, they put a perfect plot together, a conspiracy to ensnare Daniel. It backfired and they ended up as dinner for very starved and hungry lions.

> It pleased Darius to appoint 120 satraps to rule throughout the kingdom, with three administrators over them, one of whom was Daniel. The satraps were made accountable to them so that the king might not suffer loss. Now Daniel so distinguished himself among the administrators and the satraps by his exceptional qualities that the king planned to set him over the whole kingdom. At this, the administrators and the satraps tried to find grounds for charges against Daniel in his conduct of government affairs, but they were unable to do so. They could find no corruption in him, because he was trustworthy and neither corrupt nor negligent. Finally these men said, "We will never find any basis for charges against this man Daniel unless it has something to do with the law of his God." So these administrators and satraps went as a group to the king and said: "May King Darius live forever! The royal administrators, prefects, satraps, advisers and governors have all agreed that the king should issue an edict and enforce the decree that anyone who prays to any god or human being during the next thirty days, except to you, Your Majesty, shall be thrown into the lions' den. Now, Your Majesty, issue the decree and put it in writing so that it cannot be altered—in accordance with the law of the Medes and Persians, which cannot be repealed." So King Darius put the decree in writing…Then they said to the king, "Daniel, who is one of the exiles from Judah, pays no attention to you, Your Majesty, or to the decree you put in writing. He still prays three times a day." When the king heard this, he was greatly distressed; he was determined to rescue Daniel and made every effort until sundown to

save him. Then the men went as a group to King Darius and said to him, "Remember, Your Majesty, that according to the law of the Medes and Persians no decree or edict that the king issues can be changed." So the king gave the order, and they brought Daniel and threw him into the lions' den. The king said to Daniel, "May your God, whom you serve continually, rescue you!"

—DANIEL 6:1–9, 13–16, NIV

At the king's command, the men who had falsely accused Daniel were brought in and thrown into the lions' den, along with their wives and children; "And before they reached the floor of the den, the lions overpowered them and crushed all their bones" (v. 24, NIV). God is not mocked your sin will find you out (Gal. 6:9; Num. 32:23b).

Miriam

Remember the story in Numbers 12 when Aaron and Miriam speaking behind Moses' back? Well, Miriam ended up with leprosy. First Chronicles 16:22 warns, "Touch not mine anointed, and do my prophets no harm." In the New Testament Paul warns, "Rebuke not an elder, but intreat him as a father; and the younger men as brethren...Against an elder receive not an accusation, but before two or three witnesses" (1 Timothy 5:1, 19).

Death and life are in the power of the tongue: and they that love it shall eat the fruit thereof.

—PROVERBS 18:21

That means gossip kills and murders, and it does not have a place in the kingdom of God.

Now the doings (practices) of the flesh are clear:...Envy, drunkenness, carousing, and the like. I warn you beforehand, just as I did previously, that those who do such things shall not inherit the kingdom of God.

—GALATIANS 5:19A, 21, AMP

But the fearful, and unbelieving, and the abominable, and murderers, and whoremongers, and sorcerers, and idolaters, and all liars, shall have their part in the lake which burneth with fire and brimstone: which is the second death.

—REVELATION 21:8

Accountability

Jesus taught of a day of accountability for every idle word that the believer "allows" to fall from His lips.

> But I tell you that everyone will have to give account on the day of judgment for every empty word they have spoken. For by your words you will be acquitted, and by your words you will be condemned.
>
> —Matthew 12:36–37, niv

I used the word *allow* because it's a choice.

> Keep your heart with all diligence, For out of it spring the issues of life. Put away from you a deceitful mouth, And put perverse lips far from you.
>
> —Proverbs 4:23–24, nkjv

Also the Book of Colossians says you can—yes, you can—and should direct your speech with grace and well-seasoned words.

> Let your speech be always with grace, seasoned with salt, that ye may know how ye ought to answer every man.
>
> —Colossians 4:6

Paul admonished us all on how to conduct our speech in Titus 3:2: "To speak evil of no man, to be no brawlers, but gentle, shewing all meekness unto all men."

> Judge not, that ye be not judged. For with what judgment ye judge, ye shall be judged: and with what measure ye mete, it shall be measured to you again.
>
> —Matthew 7:1–2

Are you a captive of gossip? Do you find yourself entertaining gossip or in the company of gossipers? Do gossipers find it easy to approach you because you easily give hearing ears? Is your name coming up easily in the ranks of gossipers? Feast on the prophecy of Isaiah and let it be your testimony.

The Sovereign Lord has given me a well-instructed tongue, to know the word that sustains the weary, He wakens me morning by morning, wakens my ear to listen like one being instructed.

—Isaiah 50:4, NIV

By God's grace you can do it!

Jesus spoke of dealing with sin in the church:

If your brother or sister sins go and point out their fault, just between the two of you. If they listen to you, you have won them over. But if they will not listen, take one or two others along, so that "every matter may be established by the testimony of two or three witnesses." If they still refuse to listen, tell it to the church; and if they refuse to listen even to the church, treat them as you would a pagan or a tax collector.

—Matthew 18:15–17, NIV

Apostle Paul demonstrated this when he had an issue with Peter concerning certain doctrinal matters. "But when Peter was come to Antioch, I withstood him to the face, because he was to be blamed" (Gal. 2:11)—not behind his back, but to his face. Several years later, Peter had this to say about the wisdom with which Paul conducted himself:

Bear in mind that our Lord's patience means salvation, just as our dear brother Paul also wrote you with the wisdom that God gave him. He writes the same way in all his letters, speaking in them of these matters. His letters contain some things that are hard to understand, which ignorant and unstable people distort, as they do the other Scriptures, to their own destruction.

—2 Peter 3:15–16, NIV

Jesus is our ultimate example in all things. We must follow His principles in handling the affairs of life. "And are built upon the foundation of the apostles and prophets, Jesus Christ himself being the chief corner stone" (Eph. 2:20). These early apostles who laid a strong foundation for us also entertained open rebuke, being mindful of each other's ranking in the Lord. Proverbs 27:5 drives the point home for all generations: "Better is open rebuke than hidden love" (NIV).

I admonish you to escape the trap of gossip now. May the curse be broken in the mighty name of Jesus Christ Son of the living God!

He who goes about as a talebearer reveals secrets; there-
fore associate not with him who talks too freely.
[PROVERBS 20:19, AMP]

You shall not go up and down as a dispenser of gossip and scandal
among your people, nor shall you [secure yourself by false testimony
or by silence and] endanger the life of your neighbor. I am the Lord.
[LEVITICUS 19:16, AMP]

Chapter 8

GENERATIONAL CURSES

MOST PEOPLE ARGUE over the authenticity of generational curses. They quote:

> The soul that sins, it [is the one that] shall die. The son shall not bear and be punished for the iniquity of the father, neither shall the father bear and be punished for the iniquity of the son; the righteousness of the righteous shall be upon him only, and the wickedness of the wicked shall be upon the wicked only.
>
> —EZEKIEL 18:20, AMP

A careful study of this scripture will reveal that it's in reference to where one spends eternity to bear the consequences of the choices we make in life. Generational curses are very real, and they pass on from one generation to the other based on sin and iniquity. It is the curse that passes from ancestors to descendants.

SIN AND INIQUITY

The sins and iniquities of the fathers are evil seeds sown in the past. Because they were not uprooted and destroyed, they have taken root downward and bear fruit upward. The fruit, which is the harvest, is what is visited upon subsequent and newer generations. Archbishop Duncan Williams said, "The snake that Adam failed to conquer or defeat in the Garden of Eden grew to become a dragon in Revelation 12."[1]

Now this is a good analogy for our studies on generational curses. Everything you do in this life is a seed. The iniquity of the fathers was a seed sown probably in the hour of ignorance. Those seeds have taken root and have become strongholds bearing all manner of evil fruit threatening to destroy the present generation.

Satan, the devil, is behind every evil. He preys on the ignorance of people to achieve his diabolical goals. He positions behind-the-scenes forces that enforce the curse down many generations. Many have gone to their grave early, never fulfilling purpose and destiny, because of ignorance.

> My people are destroyed for lack of knowledge: because thou hast rejected knowledge, I will also reject thee, that thou shalt be no priest to me: seeing thou hast forgotten the law of thy God, I will also forget thy children.
>
> —HOSEA 4:6

> Lest Satan should get an advantage of us: for we are not ignorant of his devices.
>
> —2 CORINTHIANS 2:11

The devil has never changed his ways or his mission—to steal, kill, and destroy.

> The thief cometh not, but for to steal, and to kill, and to destroy.
>
> —JOHN 10:10

If you remain ignorant he will wipe out your generation and turn to your children in their season of vulnerability. I encourage you to rise, take up your weapons, run into the battle, and fight, breaking the curses of your ancestral background.

You can do it!

Hedge of protection or open doors

Satan could not touch Job because of the hedge of protection around him.

> Then Satan answered the Lord, Does Job [reverently] fear God for nothing? Have You not put a hedge about him and his house and all that he has, on every side? You have conferred prosperity and happiness upon him in the work of his hands, and his possessions have increased in the land.
>
> —JOB 1:9–10, AMP

You are also under covering and God's protection because the scriptures make that clear.

He that dwelleth in the secret place of the most High shall abide under the shadow of the Almighty. I will say of the LORD, He is my refuge and my fortress: my God; in him will I trust. Surely he shall deliver thee from the snare of the fowler, and from the noisome pestilence. He shall cover thee with his feathers, and under his wings shalt thou trust: his truth shall be thy shield and buckler. Thou shalt not be afraid for the terror by night; nor for the arrow that flieth by day; Nor for the pestilence that walketh in darkness; nor for the destruction that wasteth at noonday. A thousand shall fall at thy side, and ten thousand at thy right hand; but it shall not come nigh thee. Only with thine eyes shalt thou behold and see the reward of the wicked. Because thou hast made the LORD, which is my refuge, even the most High, thy habitation; There shall no evil befall thee, neither shall any plague come nigh thy dwelling.

—PSALM 91:1-10

There is a hedge of protection over and around the believers. But the Bible also teaches us that anyone who breaks the hedge opens the door, creating an opening for the serpent to come in and bite. "He that diggeth a pit shall fall into it; and whoso breaketh an hedge, a serpent shall bite him" (Eccles. 10:8).

The devil is an opportunist, he will gladly step into any door you open ignorantly or innocently and take advantage of everyone within the house.

The scriptures are very clear: "Neither give place to the devil" (Eph. 4:27). Any door opened by the ancestors gave Satan a foothold and has allowed the serpent to come in and bite.

In physics, it is said, "Every object continues in its state of rest, or of motion in a straight line at constant speed, unless it is compelled to change that state by forces exerted on it."[2]

Have you ever seen a movie where some guy knocks on a lady's door? She may not want to open the door, but she cracks it just a little bit to get a word out and immediately the guy puts his foot in and then forces the door open. Now that is how Satan operates. You give him an inch, and he will come in and occupy and dominate.

Many believers claim exemption from generational curses without breaking the curses. Neither do they take the time to visit the root of the curse to deal with it. They conveniently quote scriptures like, "Therefore if any man be in Christ, he is a new creature: old things are passed away; behold all things are become new" (2 Cor. 5:17).

Many brush off the subject by saying *they* didn't do it. Well, it might interest you to know that in the realm of the spirit, Satan does not entertain explanation. "I was not there when it took place," does not move him. God admonished Israel through the prophet Isaiah to go back to their roots.

> Listen to Me, you who follow after righteousness, You who seek the LORD; Look to the rock from which you were hewn, And to the hole of the pit from which you were dug. Look to Abraham your father, And to Sarah who bore you; For I called him alone, And blessed him and increased him.
>
> —ISAIAH 51:1–2, NKJV

> For whatsoever things were written aforetime were written for our learning, that we through patience and comfort of the scriptures might have hope.
>
> —ROMANS 15:4

It's time to go back to your roots to research who your ancestors were. Research their trade, covenants, religion, beliefs, and lifestyles.

What seeds have they sown? Do you have a murderer as an ancestor? Did anybody shed innocent blood on purpose or by accident? Was anybody into idolatry or partake in destroying the work of God (church, ministries) or rebelled against a servant of God? Has anyone destroyed someone's marriage or been an accomplice in destroying their neighbor? Did anyone steal God's money? These and many more actions could open the door for generational curses.

Until somebody rises to shut that door with the necessary force and drive the serpent out, it will continue to travel down that bloodline biting innocent and ignorant victims.

GENEALOGIES AND FAMILY TREES

Have you ever wondered why God put genealogies in the Bible? Even though the greater majority of believers skip genealogies in scripture, God has hidden treasures in the genealogies and He wants us to seek them out just like the children of Israel knew their ancestors.

You also have a genealogy or family tree, and it is wisdom to seek it out and to know the personalities of your bloodline because this could hold the clue to some of the unexplained negative occurrences in your life, peradventure there is a curse. This is especially important if you are experiencing a virtuous cycle of negativities, near-success syndrome, failures, stubborn chronic diseases, prevailing poverty, humiliation, oppression, barrenness, unfruitfulness, etc.

When you look at your siblings, parents, grandparents do you see a pattern of certain prevailing bloodline issues. Do you see your family (bloodline) in the light of the Book of Numbers?

> The LORD is longsuffering, and of great mercy, forgiving iniquity and transgression, and by no means clearing the guilty, visiting the iniquity of the fathers upon the children unto the third and fourth generation.
>
> —NUMBERS 14:18

Your family may be seriously wounded by the curse caused by the iniquity of the fathers. How are you treating the wound?

> For they have healed the hurt of the daughter of my people slightly, saying, Peace, peace; when there is no peace. Were they ashamed when they had committed abomination? nay, they were not at all ashamed, neither could they blush: therefore shall they fall among them that fall: in the time of their visitation they shall be cast down, saith the LORD. I will surely consume them, saith the LORD: there shall be no grapes on the vine, nor figs on the fig tree, and the leaf shall fade; and the things that I have given them shall pass away from them. Why do we sit still? assemble yourselves, and let us enter into the defenced cities, and let us be silent there: for the LORD our God hath put us to silence, and given us water of gall to drink, because we have sinned against the LORD. We looked for peace, but no good came; and for a time of health, and behold trouble! The snorting of his horses was heard from Dan: the whole land trembled at the sound of the neighing of his strong ones; for they are come, and have devoured the land, and all that is in it; the city, and those that dwell therein. For, behold, I will send serpents, cockatrices, among you, which will not be charmed, and they shall bite you, saith the LORD.
>
> —JEREMIAH 8:11–17

I believe the reason God placed this book in your hands is because He has chosen you—yes, *you*—to stop the devil and all his agents now and break the curse in your bloodline and dress the family wound.

Defining moment of a Moabite woman

One of the most accursed nations of the ancient world was Moab. Their abominable ways provoked several prophets to pronounce curses upon the nation; among them were Isaiah, Jeremiah, Ezekiel, Amos, and Nehemiah.

In Deuteronomy 23 God brought judgment upon Moab through His servant Moses forbidding the Ammonites and Moabites from entering into the assembly of the Lord. They practiced idolatry, prostitution, and demonic sacrifices including human sacrifice to Chemosh, their idol god. They indulged in very deplorable high levels of immorality, just to name a few.

In fact, Moab came into existence through the illicit, incestuous relationship between Lot and his two daughters after the fall of Sodom. Lot named the child Moab who was born to him by his oldest daughter (Gen. 19:37).

During the Exodus of Israel from Egypt, the king of Moab, Balak, hired Balaam, a man who practiced divination to curse Israel. But when this failed, Balak said he could not curse whom God has blessed (Num. 23:8, 20).

In the process of time, Ruth, a Moabites woman, contacted grace that changed her life and destiny for all eternity. She broke the curse of her bloodline when she entered into covenant with the God of mercy and second chances. The defining moment that changed her life is recorded in the book named after her. "Don't urge me to leave you or to turn back from you. Where you go I will go, and where you stay I will stay. Your people will be my people and your God my God" (Ruth 1:16, NIV).

As a result of this covenant, God brought Boaz into her life. Interestingly, Boaz also had some skeletons in his closet; his parents were Rahab the harlot of Jericho and Salmon, one of the two spies she helped to escape the wrath of her people. She broke every curse she may have incurred through prostitution when she helped the spies escape and entered into covenant with God. (See Joshua 2:1–24.) The union of Ruth and Boaz produced Obed, who gave birth to Jesse, who gave birth to David the king, who became the great-ancestor of Jesus Christ our Savior.

Through the covenant of Ruth, God brought two very bitter enemy nations—Moab and Israel—together to produce the Messiah.

Your turn

It is never too late to experience God's best for your life. He can do anything! That is why you should not allow any curse to hold you down and reduce you to the status where you dwell and play with chickens. You have an eagle in you; break every curse and limitation on your potential, rise from where you are, and begin to fly and soar above every mountain, together with the Holy Spirit. No storm can stop you. God promised through His prophet Isaiah:

> Also the sons of the stranger, that join themselves to the LORD, to serve him, and to love the name of the LORD, to be his servants, every one that keepeth the sabbath from polluting it, and taketh hold of my covenant; Even them will I bring to my holy mountain, and make them joyful in my house of prayer: their burnt offerings and their sacrifices shall be accepted upon mine altar; for mine house shall be called an house of prayer for all people.
>
> —ISAIAH 56:6–7

Don't relent, you've got the power!

That curse has a cause, find it and deal with it before it deals with you. "As the bird by wandering, as the swallow by flying, so the curse causeless shall not come" (Prov. 26:2).

You are the generation that seeks the Lord: "This is the generation of them that seek him that seek thy face, O Jacob. Selah" (Ps. 24:6).

You are the generation that tells the devil enough is enough.

Read the incredible prayer of Jeremiah for restoration.

> Remember, O LORD, what is come upon us: consider, and behold our reproach. Our inheritance is turned to strangers, our houses to aliens. We are orphans and fatherless, our mothers are as widows. We have drunken our water for money; our wood is sold unto us. Our necks are under persecution: we labor, and have no rest. We have given the hand to the Egyptians, and to the Assyrians, to be satisfied with bread. Our fathers have sinned, and are not; and we

have borne their iniquities. Servants have ruled over us: there is none that doth deliver us out of their hand. We gat our bread with the peril of our lives because of the sword of the wilderness. Our skin was black like an oven because of the terrible famine. They ravished the women in Zion, and the maids in the cities of Judah. Princes are hanged up by their hand: the faces of elders were not honoured. They took the young men to grind, and the children fell under the wood. The elders have ceased from the gate, the young men from their musick. The joy of our heart is ceased; our dance is turned into mourning. The crown is fallen from our head: woe unto us that we have sinned! For this our heart is faint; for these things our eyes are dim. Because of the mountain of Zion, which is desolate, the foxes walk upon it.

—LAMENTATIONS 5:1–18

Does this scripture hit home? Is this reality for you? Can you iden-tify with the pain of the remnant of Israel as the prophet led them in prayer to pour their hearts out before the Lord? There is hope, child of God; yes, there is hope for you.

The testimony of "what mean ye, that ye use this proverb concerning the land of Israel, saying, The fathers have eaten sour grapes, and the children's teeth are set on edge?" (Ezek. 18:2) shall *not* be your portion. It shall only remain a proverb, by the grace of God. By the sustainable hand of the Lord upon your life and underneath you as you press your way to discover and recover, you can break the generational curse in your bloodline and "the gates of hell shall not prevail" (Matt. 16:18b).

Read Isaiah 58:11–12 out loud.

And the LORD shall guide thee continually, and satisfy thy soul in drought, and make fat thy bones: and thou shalt be like a watered garden, and like a spring of water, whose waters fail not. And they that shall be of thee shall build the old waste places: thou shalt raise up the foundations of many generations; and thou shalt be called, The repairer of the breach, The restorer of paths to dwell in.

Yes, by *your* hand the Lord will build the old waste places; you will repair the breach caused by your ancestors. You will also restore paths to dwell in. You will lay a better foundation for the generation after you.

You can do it! Until you rise, your family will continue to be hypnotized under the sway of the wicked one.

> And we know that we are of God, and the whole world lieth in wickedness.
> —1 JOHN 5:19

Until you rise, Satan will not open the prison doors where he has kept your family hostage.

> [Satan] made the world as a wilderness, and destroyed the cities thereof; that opened not the house of his prisoners.
> —ISAIAH 14:17

Until you rise, Satan will continue to be the strongman. But when you rise, you become the stronger man.

> When a strong man armed keepeth his palace, his goods are in peace.
> —LUKE 11:21

Until you rise to shut the mouth of iniquity, the poor will not have hope.

> He saveth the poor from the sword, from their mouth, and from the hand of the mighty. So the poor hath hope, and iniquity stoppeth her mouth
> —JOB 5:15–16

Until you rise, he will continue to enforce poverty, calamities, tragedies, marital failures, bareness, disfavor, etc., in your bloodline. Be that generation that takes a stand in God to declare, "No more!"

> In those days they shall say *no more*, The fathers have eaten a sour grape, and the children's teeth are set on edge.
> —JER. 31:29A, EMPHASIS ADDED

No more!
In the next chapter, we will identify some of the most common doors opened by the iniquity of the ancestors.

*He who works deceit shall not dwell in my house; he
who tells lies shall not continue in my presence.*
[PSALM 101:7, AMP]

*Truthful lips shall be established forever, but a lying
tongue is [credited] but for a moment.*
[PROVERBS 12:19, AMP]

Chapter 9
LIES

As the bird by wandering, as the swallow by flying,
so the curse causeless shall not come.
—Proverbs 26:2

ABRAHAM OPENED THE door to lies. This spirit stayed in his bloodline for many generations. Even though some Bible scholars argue that Sarah was related to Abraham and therefore he was justified by calling her sister, truth remains that Sarah was married to him. Out of fear for his life, he lied about their marriage and said Sarah was his sister.

> So Pharaoh summoned Abram. "What have you done to me?" he said. "Why didn't you tell me she was your wife? Why did you say, 'She is my sister,' so that I took her to be my wife? Now then, here is your wife. Take her and go!
> —GENESIS 12:18–19, NIV

As if once was not enough, he repeated this same episode in Gerar.

> And Abraham said of Sarah his wife, She is my sister: and Abimelech king of Gerar sent, and took Sarah.
> —GENESIS 20:2

I wonder how Sarah felt—maybe betrayed, belittled, and ashamed? We may never know. Did this affect their marriage? At the time of these two incidents, Isaac was not yet born; but the seed had already been sown.

ISAAC

> And the men of the place asked him of his wife; and he said, She is my sister: for he feared to say, She is my wife; lest, said he, the

men of the place should kill me for Rebekah; because she was
fair to look upon.

—Genesis 26:7

Isaac also ended up in Gerar and for fear for his life, and he did
exactly what the previous generation did (His father, Abraham). How
did he know or learn to do that? The proverb says, "Like father, like
son."

Jacob and His Sons

Jacob is now the third generation of Abraham's bloodline, and one
might say it runs in the blood. Jacob lied to his blind father in his old
age and got the blessing of the firstborn. Read the story in Genesis
27:18–24.

This incident divided the brothers; it drew a wedge between them.
When Esau threatened to kill Jacob, he took refuge with his Uncle
Laban in Haran. (See Genesis 27:41–45.) Jacob later had twelve sons,
and ten of them continued the lies of the bloodline. While in his old
age, at a time when he should be enjoying retirement benefits, ten of
his sons conspired and lied to him about the death of Joseph, the son
he loved the most. They dipped his coat of many colors in blood and
lied to their father that Joseph was killed by wild animals.

> Then they got Joseph's robe, slaughtered a goat and dipped the
> robe in the blood. They took the ornate robe back to their father
> and said, "We found this. Examine it to see whether it is your
> son's robe." He recognized it and said, "It is my son's robe! Some
> ferocious animal has devoured him. Joseph has surely been torn
> to pieces." Then Jacob tore his clothes, put on sackcloth and
> mourned for his son many days. All his sons and daughters came
> to comfort him, but he refused to be comforted. "No," he said, "I
> will continue to mourn until I join my son in the grave." So his
> father wept for him. Meanwhile, the Midianites sold Joseph in
> Egypt to Potiphar, one of Pharaoh's officials, the captain of the
> guard.
>
> —Genesis 37:31–36, niv

For twenty years they comforted the old man with lies, knowing
very well that they sold Joseph into slavery. Can you picture the old

gray-headed patriarch, tossing and turning in his bed, crying himself to sleep night after night? Picture him restless in his tent, languishing in pain, wounded and sorrowing in his heart. See him continually asking, "Why did this happen to me?" First he lost Rachel, the woman he loved most, and then Joseph, the son of his heart. Well, he wouldn't have to look too far. The proverb says, "An apple does not fall far from the tree." The long arm of the past is just catching up to him. The sins (lies) of his forefathers have finally caught up with him at a time when he least expected it. Oh, what a terrible price to pay for lying!

Joseph walked in truth. He refused to compromise his faith. By the spirit of holiness and integrity of heart, he broke the lying curse of the Abrahamic bloodline. He refused to harbor bitterness and resentment in his heart towards those who did him harm by wrongfully accusing and lying about him to defame and assassinate his character. He was able to discern and identify human error and mistakes from demonic calculations and satanic agenda designed to entrap and derail his purpose. He demonstrated godly love through forgiveness. This example is very much needed in the church and family cycle today.

DECEPTION OF THE GIBEONITES

The Gibeonites once came to Joshua in disguise and used the name of the Lord to deceive him by lying. Deception got them through the door, but great was their fall! In the kingdom of God, there is no substitute for honesty and integrity. Jesus said, "Let your 'Yes' be 'Yes'" (Matt. 5:37, NKJV).

Every time you engage the tools of the devil, there will be a terrible price to pay.

Satan is the master strategist of deception. As people of God, we must be conscious of his devices. His ways may look good in the beginning, but they will lead you into destruction.

> Then they went to Joshua in the camp at Gilgal and said to him and the Israelites, "We have come from a distant country; make a treaty with us." The Israelites said to the Hivites, "But perhaps you live near us, so how can we make a treaty with you?" "We are your servants," they said to Joshua. But Joshua asked, "Who are you and where do you come from?" They answered: "Your servants have come from a very distant country because of the

fame of the LORD your God. For we have heard reports of him: all that he did in Egypt, [10] and all that he did to the two kings of the Amorites east of the Jordan—Sihon king of Heshbon, and Og king of Bashan, who reigned in Ashtaroth. And our elders and all those living in our country said to us, 'Take provisions for your journey; go and meet them and say to them, "We are your servants; make a treaty with us."'

—JOSHUA 9:6–11, NIV

The Gibeonites succeeded in their deception because Joshua did not consult with the Lord before going into league with them.

Truth cannot be hidden always.

Within three days, they were exposed and great was the curse they incurred through the old general and spiritual leader (authority figure) Joshua. "Now therefore ye are cursed, and there shall none of you be freed from being bondmen, and hewers of wood and drawers of water for the house of my God" (Josh. 9:23). To this day, the word of God declares it is so according to the word of Joshua.

And Joshua made them that day hewers of wood and drawers of water for the congregation, and for the altar of the LORD, even unto this day, in the place which he should choose.

—JOSHUA 9:27

SEXUAL PERVERSION

Without wanting to sound judgmental or "holier than thou," I must tell you that sexual perversion is an abomination before the Lord. The Hebrew word from which we get the translation of "perverted persons" is *qedeshim*, meaning those practicing sodomy and prostitution in rituals. The Bible is very clear about the curse incurred by those who are into this practice and the ripple effect it has on subsequent generations.

Adultery, fornication, homosexuality, lesbianism, incest, child molestation, and rape, just to name a few, are open doors for the spirits of lust and immorality that eventually pass on to the next generation.

Judah

In Genesis 38:1–30 we read of Judah, the fourth son of Jacob, who lost two sons and blamed it on his daughter-in-law instead of correcting the wrong done in his household. He sent the woman away with a promise he had no intention of keeping. This later came back to haunt and hurt him. He traveled to another town where he spent the night in the arms of a prostitute. The harlot turned out to be Tamar, the daughter-in-law he sent away with a lie. She conceived and bore him twins, Perez and Zarah.

The scale of God's mercy is beyond anybody's comprehension.

God turned the mistake and sin of Judah into a miracle. In Matthew 1:2–6 we read how this bloodline became the genealogy that produced David and eventually the Messiah. God's mercy can change your story into a blessing if you will accept it with true repentance.

Jesus said, "The scripture cannot be broken" (John 10:35b). Because the union between Judah and Tamar was a forbidden marriage, it made their children bastards until the tenth generation: "A bastard shall not enter into the congregation of the LORD; even to his tenth generation shall he not enter into the congregation of the LORD" (Deut. 23:2). So, ten generations had to pay the price for Judah's illicit sex encounter. The tenth generation ended with Jesse, father of David.

Saul became king over God's people even though he was a Benjamite. The right to kingship was given to Judah. Is it possible that Jesse could have been the first king, but because of Judah and Tamar's sin he was denied access?

David

David was doing fine until the night he chose to stay home instead of being on the battlefield. He saw something he could not resist. A seed of sexual perversion that had been lying dormant for ten generations rose like a giant within him. He committed adultery with Bathsheba, the wife of Uriah the Hittite, a faithful servant in his army. David killed him and then married Bathsheba. David later repented, and the mercy of God changed their testimony by giving them Solomon the King. Read the entire chapter of 2 Samuel 11.

The hedge was broken ten generations earlier, and the serpent remained in the bloodline biting subsequent generations. Ecclesiastes 10:8 declares, "He that diggeth a pit shall fall into it: and whoso breaketh an hedge, a serpent shall bite him."

David's son Amnon could not resist his own sister; he faked sickness and raped her when she brought him food at his request (see

2 Samuel 13:1–20). Absalom also committed adultery with his father, David's, concubines in the open, all in one day.

> And Ahithophel said unto Absalom. Go in unto thy father's concubines, which he hath left to keep the house; and all Israel shall hear that thou art abhorred of thy father: then shall the hands of all that that are with thee be strong. So they spread Absalom a tent upon the top of the house; and Absalom went in unto his father's concubines in the sight of all Israel.
>
> —2 SAMUEL 6:21–22

These acts fulfilled the word of the Lord by the prophet Nathan:

> Thus saith the LORD, Behold, I will raise up evil against thee out of thine own house, and I will take thy wives before thine eyes, and give them unto thy neighbour, and he shall lie with thy wives in the sight of this sun.
>
> —2 SAMUEL 12:11

Solomon

The seed of immorality sown in the days of Judah had now taken strong root downward, and Solomon lost control in this area of his life despite his wisdom.

> And the LORD was angry with Solomon, because his heart was turned from the LORD God of Israel, which had appeared unto him twice. And had commanded him concerning this thing that he should not go after other gods: but he kept not that which the LORD commanded.
>
> —1 KINGS 11:9–10

God appeared to Solomon twice and warned him regarding these things; but after many years, he could no longer resist the temptation.

> But King Solomon loved many strange women, together with the daughter Pharaoh, women of the Moabites, Ammonites, Edomites, Zidonians and Hivites. Of the nations concerning which the LORD said unto the children of Israel, ye shall not go in to them neither shall they come in unto you: for surely they will turn your hearts after their gods: Solomon clave unto these in love. And he had

seven hundred wives, princesses, and three hundred concubines: and his wives turned away his heart.

—1 KINGS 11:1–3

He married one thousand women who turned his heart from the Lord and made him use God's money and resources to build high places (worship temples) for their idol gods. What tragedy! What a price to pay for lust and immorality! This became the root cause for the divided kingdom of Israel in the next generation.

Wherefore the LORD said unto Solomon, Forasmuch as this is done of thee, and thou hast not kept my covenant and my statutes, which I have commanded thee, I will surely rend the kingdom from thee, and will give it to thy servant. Notwithstanding in thy days I will not do it for David thy father's sake: but I will rend it out of the hand of thy son. Howbeit I will not rend away all the kingdom; but will give one tribe to thy son for David my servant's sake, and for Jerusalem's sake which I have chosen.

—1 KINGS 11:11–13

Look at verse 14: "And the LORD stirred up an adversary unto Solomon, Hadad the Edomite: he was of the king's seed in Edom." Adversaries were raised against him.

In his later years, Solomon expressed his regrets, time and again, in the Book of Ecclesiastes. He said it was all "vanity upon vanities" (Eccles. 1:2). Solomon died young—about sixty years of age. I guess disobedience and one thousand women calling you husband can send you to an early grave. The apostle Paul admonished the believers to flee youthful lust (2 Tim. 2:22).

Joseph broke the curse

Joseph broke this curse in his bloodline when he said no to Potiphar's wife by turning down her seducing advances.

And after a while his master's wife took notice of Joseph and said, "Come to bed with me!" But he refused. "With me in charge," he told her, "my master does not concern himself with anything in the house; everything he owns he has entrusted to my care. No one is greater in this house than I am. My master has withheld nothing from me except you, because you are his wife. How then could I do such a wicked thing and sin against God?" And though she spoke to Joseph day after day, he refused to go to bed with her or even be with her. One day he went into the house to attend to his duties, and none of the household servants was inside. She caught him by his cloak and said, "Come to bed with me!" But he left his cloak in her hand and ran out of the house.

—GENESIS 39:7–12, NIV

Consider verse 9 where he demonstrated his fear and love for God and his appreciation for the favor with Potiphar. Run, child of God, and don't leave anything behind for Potiphar's wife to accuse you by! Please run, and start running now!

CURSE ON THE FAMILY NAME

There are many people ignorantly walking around and laboring under curses based on their family name, names conferred upon them by ancestors with the accompanying curses that passed on to the present generation. Some of these names were invoked during demonic covenants and rituals; others are names that honor deities of the demonic kingdom.

However these names came about, many have become captives and victims of the behind-the-scenes forces, controlling powers planted as messengers of darkness to enforce the curse that these names mean and carry. This is one of many reasons why it is advisable, especially for those who may feel like victims caught up in the negative occurrence in their respective families, to research and know who your ancestors were and how the family name came about. Ancestry.com is an official site that has helped many discover their genealogy; it may be a good place to start your search. They have genealogy records including censuses that could be of great help.

There are many names also that some parents gave to their children at birth that have a direct negative impact on the life and destiny of the child. Some have carelessly named and invoked curses upon their children as a result of the experiences they went through during the pregnancy and the pain at childbirth. Benjamin was the last of Israel's twelve sons, the younger of the two children he had with his beloved wife Rachel, who died while giving birth to Benjamin. Her dying words were to name the child Benoni, meaning "son of my sorrow." Jacob, being a spiritual person, understood the implications and quickly broke the curse of sorrow that could have possibly followed the child by renaming him Benjamin, meaning "son of my right hand" (Gen. 35:18). (See Genesis 35:16–20).

Israel himself had been the victim of a name that had negative impact on his nature. As the son of Isaac and Rebecca, his parents named him Jacob, meaning "holder of the heel or sup-planter." He had a twin brother. A struggle began in the womb between the twin brothers; and when they were born, the younger (Jacob) came out holding on to the heel of the older (Esau), hence the name Jacob. The Lord had told Rebecca that, contrary to the order of the day, the older would serve the younger. Jacob, as his name suggested, supplanted his brother many times to assume the role of big brother. (See Genesis 25:22–26.)

The Lord changed his name from Jacob to Israel, which signified a turning point in his life. (See Genesis 32:24–28 and Genesis 35:9–10.) Sometimes all it takes is to change the name and break the curse.

HEALING IN ZAIRE

In 2006 while holding a meeting in Zaire, a young man was carried into the prayer line. He looked very pale. Doctors had given up on him because they could not diagnose what was killing him. Before praying for him I asked for his name, which meant death in his native dialect. I had a check in my spirit that death had been following him because of his name. I asked my interpreter to translate the name "Life" into his dialect and to explain to him that the Lord was impressing upon me to change his name from death to life. When that was agreed upon, we prayed and rebuked death from following him.

The following day, a young man nicely dressed and well-groomed walked up to me in the meeting and introduced himself as Life. The curse was broken when we changed his name, and the Lord healed him for His glory. His testimony drew many to Christ.

Sometimes a name may not be a curse but a limitation in certain areas in the life of the individual that could serve as a monitoring device for the forces of darkness to pursue and accomplish their diabolical assignment. A name change can make a big difference, as in the case of God changing the name Abram to Abraham and Sarai to Sarah.

> As for Me, behold, My covenant (solemn pledge) is with you, and you shall be the father of many nations. Nor shall your name any longer be Abram [high, exalted father]; but your name shall be Abraham [father of a multitude], for I have made you the father of many nations.
> —GENESIS 17:4–5, AMP

> And God said to Abraham, As for Sarai your wife, you shall not call her name Sarai; but Sarah [Princess] her name shall be. And I will bless her and give you a son also by her. Yes, I will bless her, and she shall be a mother of nations; kings of peoples shall come from her.
> —GENESIS 17:15–16, AMP

This principle can also apply to businesses. A simple name change can be game changer between average and extraordinary.

HELPFUL SCRIPTURES

Genesis 18:20–21
Leviticus 18:22
Leviticus 20:13
1 Kings 12:25–27
Deuteronomy 23:17
Romans 1:26–27
1 Corinthians 6:9–10

My people are destroyed for lack of knowledge; because you [the priestly nation] have rejected knowledge, I will also reject you that you shall be no priest to Me; seeing you have forgotten the law of your God, I will also forget your children.
[HOSEA 4:6, AMP]

Chapter 10
INNOCENT, IGNORANT, OR DELIBERATE ACTS THAT INVOKE CURSES

THE UNGODLY CHOICE OF REUBEN

REUBEN WAS THE firstborn of Jacob. He committed an act that was deplorable and degrading in any circle of life, in any generation.

> And it came to pass, when Israel dwelt in that land, that Reuben went and lay with Bilhah his father's concubine: and Israel heard it. Now the sons of Jacob were twelve.
> —GENESIS 35:22

We live in times that make light of abominable acts of this nature. Reuben must have been morally enslaved to willfully commit adultery with his father's wife. The curse he incurred by this act would eventually devour the men of his bloodline. For a season everything seemed okay, which is where the deception lies. The fact that judgment was deferred does not mean it is okay to continue in sin.

> The Lord is not slack concerning his promise, as some men count slackness; but is longsuffering to us-ward, not willing that any should perish, but that all should come to repentance.
> —2 PETER 3:9

> And the LORD said, My spirit shall not always strive with man, for that he also is flesh: yet his days shall be an hundred and twenty years.
> —GENESIS 6:3

But this is exactly why Jesus came, and there is no sin that His precious blood cannot forgive. When Jacob was dying, he gathered his sons to give them his final blessing, predicting the future of each one.

Reuben stood before the dying Patriarch only to hear these chilling words.

> Reuben, thou art my firstborn, my might, and the beginning of my strength, the Excellency of dignity, and the excellency of power: Unstable as water, thou shalt not excel; because thou wentest up to thy father's bed; then defiledst thou it: he went up to my couch.
>
> —GENESIS 49:3–4

He heard and saw the blessing of the firstborn slip through his hands because he had no character and, therefore, could not bring his lustful desires under control.

It is worthy of note that the anointing will lift you up, but lack of character will bring you down.

The Hebrew word for "unstable" is *pahaz*. It is from the root word that describes lawlessness. The tribe of Reuben turned out to be unstable. The words of Jacob prevailed against him. Not only did he lose his birthright to Joseph (1 Chron. 5:1), the Reubenites never produced any resourceful leaders—no judges, kings nor prophets. Judah became the tribal leader.

> Judah, thou art he whom thy brethren shall praise: thy hand shall be in the neck of thine enemies; thy father's children shall bow down before thee. Judah is a lion's whelp: from the prey, my son, thou art gone up: he stooped down, he couched as a lion, and as an old lion; who shall rouse him up? The scepter shall not depart from Judah, nor a lawgiver from between his feet, until Shiloh come; and unto him shall the gathering of the people be.
>
> —GENESIS 49:8–10

Study this scripture about adultery: "But a man who commits adultery has no sense; whoever does so destroys himself. Blows and disgrace are his lot, and his shame will never be wiped away" (Prov. 6:32–33, NIV).

Reuben lacked judgment. His sin with Bilhah was lack of judgment. After their wilderness ordeal, forty years of wandering, everyone was excited to finally enter the Promised Land. The tribe of Reuben came to Moses together with the tribe of Gad and requested their inheritance be east of the Jordan River, which is outside the Promised Land. In their shortsightedness, they failed to comprehend God's promise of a land flowing with milk and honey.

> Now the children of Reuben and the children of Gad had a very great multitude of cattle: and when they saw the land of Jazer, and the land of Gilead, that, behold, the place was a place for cattle; The children of Gad and the children of Reuben came and spake unto Moses, and to Eleazar the priest, and unto the princes of the congregation, saying Ataroth, and Dibon, and Jazer, and Nimrah, and Heshbon, and Elealeh, and Shebam, and Nebo, and Beon, Even the country which the LORD smote before the congregation of Israel is a land for cattle, and thy servants have cattle: Wherefore, said they, if we have found grace in thy sight, let this land be given unto thy servants for a possession, and bring us not over Jordan. And Moses said unto the children of Gad and to the children of Reuben, Shall your brethren go to war, and shall ye sit here?
>
> —NUMBERS 32:1–6

In fact, their choice on this side (east of Jordan) could logically be argued as part of the wilderness. Their poor choice has to be the height of unstableness even in decision making. The wilderness was intended to be a temporary place, a place to pass through, not to settle down and make it a final destination. The choice of the Reubenites to settle in this region permanently was based on the deception of the vegetation of the area. The Hebrew word for wilderness is *midbar*, and it means a place for driving flocks.

In the days of Deborah and Barak, when war broke out between Israel and the Canaanites, all the other tribes produced men of war for the battle but the tribe of Reuben failed to answer the call to arms. After the victory of Israel, Deborah wrote the victory song.

> And the princes of Issachar were with Deborah; even Issachar, and also Barak: he was sent on foot into the valley. For the divisions of Reuben there were great thoughts of heart. Why abodest thou among the sheepfolds, to hear the bleatings of the flocks? For the divisions of Reuben there were great searchings of heart.
>
> —JUDGES 5:15–16

The Reubenites also participated in the erection of an unauthorized place of worship which was forbidden in Israel.

> And when they came unto the borders of Jordan, that are in the land of Canaan, the children of Reuben and the children of Gad and the half tribe of Manasseh built there an altar by Jordan, a great altar to see to. And the children of Israel heard say, Behold, the children of Reuben and the children of Gad and the half tribe of Manasseh have built an altar over against the land of Canaan, in the borders of Jordan, at the passage of the children of Israel. And when the children of Israel heard of it, the whole congregation of the children of Israel gathered themselves together at Shiloh, to go up to war against them.
>
> —JOSHUA 22:10–12

Please read the rest of this abominable act from the NIV translation.

The Moabites also lived in this region known as *Mishor* in Hebrew. They oftentimes clashed with the tribe of Reuben. This had a negative impact on their numbers. They also lived in the shadows of Gad. They were cut off by the judgment of God through Jehu.

> Yet Jehu was not careful to keep the law of the LORD, the God of Israel, with all his heart. He did not turn away from the sins of Jeroboam, which he had caused Israel to commit. In those days the LORD began to reduce the size of Israel. Hazael overpowered the Israelites throughout their territory east of the Jordan in all the land of Gilead (the region of Gad, Reuben and Manasseh), from Aroer by the Arnon Gorge through Gilead to Bashan.
>
> —2 KINGS 10:31–33, NIV

The Reubenites could not excel and they were unstable. The first census in the Book of Numbers (1:20–21) place their population at 46,500. By the second census, their number had decreased to 43,730.

> These are the families of the Reubenites: and they that were numbered of them were forty and three thousand and seven hundred and thirty.
>
> —NUMBERS 26:7

Moses was a skillful intercessor before leaving the scene. He blessed all the tribes but could not say much about Rueben. Deuteronomy 33:6 says, "Let Reuben live, and not die; and let not his men be few." He pleaded with God to let Reuben live and that his men will not be few!

> Can a man take fire in his bosom and his clothes not be burned? Can one go upon hot coals, and his feet not be burned? So he that goeth in to his neighbour's wife; whosoever toucheth her shall not be innocent.
>
> —PROVERBS 6:27–29

> Flee fornication, every sin that a man doeth is without the body; but he that committeth fornication sinneth against his own body.
>
> —1 CORINTHIANS 6:18

Your body is God's temple; keep it clean!

> What? know ye not that your body is the temple of the Holy Ghost which is in you, which ye have of God, and ye are not your own? For ye are bought with a price: therefore glorify God in your body, and in your spirit, which are God's.
>
> —1 CORINTHIANS 6:19–20

(See also Genesis 18:20–21; Leviticus 18:22; Leviticus 20:13; 1 Kings 14:24–27; Romans 1:26–27; 1 Corinthians 6:9–10; Judges 19:22; Deuteronomy 23:17; Isaiah 30:9.)

THE GREED OF SILVER AND GOLD

Embezzlement of God's money, obtaining money by wicked and crooked means, cheating innocent laborers, defrauding the saints, armed robbery, drug trafficking, and other forms of blood money could open the door to the curse of poverty to flow freely and operate without restraint. God wants us to prosper and be in good health (3 John 1:2). However, the means by which you affirm the wealth and the love for it is where the problem lies.

> But they that will be rich fall into temptation and a snare, and into many foolish and hurtful lusts, which drown men in destruction and perdition. For the love of money is the root of

all evil: which while some coveted after, they have erred from the
faith, and pierced themselves through with many sorrows.

—1 TIMOTHY 6:9–10

The family of Eli

The old high priest successfully guarded and raised Samuel the
prophet, but he failed miserably in chastising his own children,
Hophni and Phinehas. They were priests in Israel giving to greed and
covetousness. "For I have told him that I will judge his house for ever
for the iniquity which he knoweth; because his sons made themselves
vile, and he restrained them not" (1 Sam. 3:13).

They stole God's money, misused it, and used their positions of
authority to forcibly take from the people.

> Also before they burnt the fat, the priest's servant came, and said to
> the man that sacrificed, Give flesh to roast for the priest; for he will
> not have sodden flesh of thee, but raw. And if any man said unto
> him, Let them not fail to burn the fat presently, and then take as
> much as thy soul desireth; then he would answer him, Nay; but thou
> shalt give it me now: and if not, I will take it by force. Wherefore
> the sin of the young men was very great before the LORD: for men
> abhorred the offering of the LORD.
>
> —1 SAMUEL 2:15–17

They also desecrated the temple of God by sleeping with women
who came there (1 Sam. 2:22). They heaped curses upon themselves,
and generations yet unborn paid a terrible price.

Remember, in the realm of the spirit, you cannot say "I was not
there." It doesn't matter. There are many young men in the body of
Christ today, including ministers with very promising futures, who
are playing Russian roulette with their destinies by following the
example of Hophni and Phinehas. They lure unsuspecting, vulnerable
women into bed with the promise of marriage. Once they get what
they want, they dump these sisters with the excuse of "waiting on
God" and they move on to others (spiritual gigolos).

Paul tells us, "Where sin abounded, grace did much more abound"
(Rom. 5:20). Yet, the apostle didn't want anybody taking undue advan-
tage of grace to indulge in sin. Consider these questions Paul asked:
"What shall we say then? Shall we continue in sin, that grace may

abound?" (6:1). His answer is, "God forbid. How shall we, that are dead to sin, live any longer therein?" (v. 2).

The curse pronounced on the house of Eli and subsequent generations should serve as a "wake-up call" to all who call upon the name of the Lord.

> Therefore the LORD, the God of Israel, declares: "I promised that members of your family would minister before me forever." But now the LORD declares: "Far be it from me! Those who honor me I will honor, but those who despise me will be disdained. The time is coming when I will cut short your strength and the strength of your priestly house, so that no one in it will reach old age, and you will see distress in my dwelling. Although good will be done to Israel, no one in your family line will ever reach old age. Every one of you that I do not cut off from serving at my altar I will spare only to destroy your sight and sap your strength, and all your descendants will die in the prime of life. And what happens to your two sons, Hophni and Phinehas, will be a sign to you—they will both die on the same day. I will raise up for myself a faithful priest, who will do according to what is in my heart and mind. I will firmly establish his priestly house, and they will minister before my anointed one always. Then everyone left in your family line will come and bow down before him for a piece of silver and a loaf of bread and plead, 'Appoint me to some priestly office so I can have food to eat.'"
>
> —1 SAMUEL 2:30–36, NIV

Let's break this down for further understanding:

- Lifespan cut short
- Enemies afflict them at ease
- Banned from leadership positions in the house of God
- Affliction of poverty
- Distress
- Premature death
- Some left alive to witness the ruin of the family
- "The scripture cannot be broken" (John 10:35b)

- The curse quietly began to devour the family of Eli

Look at the sequence:

1. The two sons of Eli died the same day in battle: "And
   the ark of God was taken; and the two sons of Eli,
   Hophni and Phinehas, were slain" (1 Sam. 4:11).

2. Upon hearing the news that the ark of God was captured, the ninety-eight-year-old father (Eli) fell backward from his seat, broke his neck, and died.

   > And it came to pass, when he made mention of the
   > ark of God, that he fell from off the seat backward by
   > the side of the gate, and his neck brake, and he died:
   > for he was an old man, and heavy. And he had judged
   > Israel forty years.
   >
   > —1 SAMUEL 4:18

3. The wife of Phinehas, upon hearing the news, went into
   labor and delivered a premature baby. She named the
   baby Ichabod, meaning "the glory has departed from
   Israel." Phinehas died soon after.

   > And his daughter in law, Phinehas' wife, was with
   > child, near to be delivered: and when she heard the
   > tidings that the ark of God was taken, and that her
   > father in law and her husband were dead, she bowed
   > herself and travailed; for her pains came upon her.
   > And about the time of her death the women that stood
   > by her said unto her, Fear not; for thou hast born a
   > son. But she answered not, neither did she regard it.
   > And she named the child Ichabod, saying, The glory
   > is departed from Israel: because the ark of God was
   > taken, and because of her father in law and her hus-
   > band. And she said, The glory is departed from Israel:
   > for the ark of God is taken.
   >
   > —1 SAMUEL 4:19–22

4. In the days of King David, Abiathar, a descendant of Eli,
   served as a priest. He carried the ark of God and shared
   in the hardships of David. He seemed to have succeeded

as priest for a season. But towards the end of David's life, Abiathar teamed up with Adonijah, Solomon's big brother, thinking he might be the next king: "And he conferred with Joab the son of Zeruiah, and with Abiathar the priest: and they following Adonijah helped him" (1 Kings 1:7).

> And the man of thine, whom I shall not cut off from mine altar, shall be to consume thine eyes, and to grieve thine heart: and all the increase of thine house shall die in the flower of their age.
>
> —1 Samuel 2:33

5. This proved to be his biggest mistake guided by the curse of the bloodline. The long arm of the past arrested him and subjected him to task (demonic manipulation).

> To Abiathar the priest the king said, "Go back to your fields in Anathoth. You deserve to die, but I will not put you to death now, because you carried the ark of the Sovereign Lord before my father David and shared all my father's hardships." So Solomon removed Abiathar from the priesthood of the Lord, fulfilling the word the Lord had spoken at Shiloh about the house of Eli.
>
> —1 Kings 2:26–27, niv

Greed continues

The curse of greed is very real; it has affected men and women great and small of all nationalities on the planet and destroyed many. It is the cause and driving force behind most *coups d'état*: "a sudden attempt by a small group of people to take over the government usually through violence."[1]

There are countless numbers killed by bloodshed through tribal wars in Third World countries because of greed. And the struggling economy of many others can be traced to the greed of some of its leaders, who by virtue of their offices have systemically robbed their countries and hidden the loot in foreign accounts. Most armed robberies and drug cartels also have their roots in greed, and there are people sitting in jailhouses because their cups are full and the curse of greed has finally caught up with them.

God has never and will never be a part of anything or anywhere greed reigns.

Greed is a destroyer; it has claimed many victims including great religious leaders both past and present. In 2 Kings 5:19–27, the Bible introduces us to a young minster by the name of Gehazi, the apprentice or servant of the prophet Elisha. After the healing of Naaman the Aramean, the prophet refused to accept any gifts from him. But Gehazi, driven by greed, went after Naaman and lied about the prophet and then took money and other valuable gifts from him and brought them into his tent. He misrepresented God and his servant to the new convert Naaman, who had just pledged his allegiance to God and entered into covenant with Him in appreciation for his healing. By the choice of his will and the content of his heart, Gehazi took the glory and credit for what God had done. He then went and lied to the prophet about his whereabouts and the gifts he took. Even though Elisha, by the prophetic gift of the word of knowledge revealed his greedy heart, he denied everything; which by interpretation is calling the prophet and Holy Spirit liars. The prophet cursed him and his bloodline with the leprosy of Naaman.

Gehazi chose material greed over the gift of God. He could have been a major prophet and a world changer. He could have succeeded Elisha and impacted his nation and generation as God's spokesperson. Instead greed reduced him to the status of a leper who lived to tell the stories of past memories. Elisha eventually died and carried his double portion anointing with him into the grave because there was no one to pass it on to. What a missed opportunity by Gehazi!

History is full of the stories of men and women who, through greed, inherited the curse. Many are still wasting away serving life sentences instead of serving their generation with their many talents. Their shocking true crime stories, showing their dark side, are now episodes on television shows and other networks and also found online. Through scams and schemes they have broken many dreams and hopes of unsuspecting hard working, innocent American citizens who they lured into fraudulent investment companies even at corporate levels.

Many have lost everything including life savings, security deposits, retirement funds, dream homes, businesses, and freedom.

Greed is a force that is always lusting for more, never satisfied until it has completely destroyed its victims. It has no conscience. It is selfish and unkind, malicious and envious. It is impatient, does not help, not giving but always taking. The American greed has claimed, derailed, and destroyed very promising political carriers. According to James chapter 5, greed is the main reason the wealth of the wicked is reserved for the righteous in the end time. The curse of greed is a terrible price to pay: loss of freedom and peace of mind, shame, embarrassment, and various types of destruction, including loss of life, are only some of that price.

LYING TO THE HOLY SPIRIT

In Acts 5:1–11 we read where the early church did not tolerate the spirit of greed to linger around because it can be contagious. Like Elisha did with Gehazi, Peter executed judgment of death upon Ananias and Sapphira because they conspired in their greed to lie to the Holy Ghost. Greed and lies in the New Testament church are against the Holy Spirit and must be dealt with before they gather momentum and affect others.

Defeat at Ai

In the Book of Joshua 7:1–26 we find where Israel suffered their first defeat in battle in the Promised Land against Ai due to the greed of one man named Achan. God withdrew His presence and Israel suffered many casualties. Joshua executed the judgment of death upon Achan's household because he knew God would not tolerate greed. It was considered sin in the camp. Greed is against the character of God; it is a taker but God is a giver.

This is the same spirit that brought the ministry of Samson to an abrupt end by wrong association with his materialistic girlfriend Delilah, who sold him out in her greed to the lords of the Philistines. It turned Balaam from being a prophet into practicing divination. Judas, in his greed, stole money from the ministry of Jesus and eventually sold his Master to His enemies, later committing suicide by hanging himself.

Please don't be the next victim of greed! Don't tolerate it and don't allow it to wrap its stranglehold around you. It can lead you to a regrettable place of no return. Greed is bait coated with the poison of doom.

The good news is that there is an antidote, a cure through repentance and accepting God's forgiveness and forgiving yourself. Then develop a love for giving. Dr. Mike Murdoch said, "Giving is proof that you have conquered greed."[2]

HELPFUL SCRIPTURES

So are the ways of every one that is greedy of gain; which taketh away the life of the owners thereof.
—PROVERBS 1:19

He that hasteth to be rich hath an evil eye, and considereth not that poverty shall come upon him.
—PROVERBS 28:22

Who being past feeling have given themselves over unto lasciviousness, to work all uncleanness with greediness.
—EPHESIANS 4:19

For the love of money is the root of all evil: which while some coveted after, they have erred from the faith, and pierced themselves through with many sorrows.
—1 TIMOTHY 6:10

Uprightness and right standing with God (moral and spiritual rectitude in every area and relation) elevate a nation, but sin is a reproach to any people.
[PROVERBS 14:34, AMP]

Blessed (happy, fortunate, to be envied) is the nation whose God is the Lord, the people He has chosen as His heritage.
[PSALM 33:12, AMP]

Chapter 11
CULTURE OF SPIRITUAL DEGRADATION

CONSIDER THESE VERSES:

> Be careful not to make a treaty with those who live in the land where you are going, or they will be a snare among you. Break down their altars, smash their sacred stones and cut down their Asherah poles. Do not worship any other god, for the LORD, whose name is Jealous, is a jealous God. "Be careful not to make a treaty with those who live in the land; for when they prostitute themselves to their gods and sacrifice to them, they will invite you and you will eat their sacrifices. And when you choose some of their daughters as wives for your sons and those daughters prostitute themselves to their gods, they will lead your sons to do the same.
>
> —EXODUS 34:12–16, NIV

> For it came to pass, when Solomon was old, that his wives turned away his heart after other gods: and his heart was not perfect with the LORD his God, as was the heart of David his father.
>
> —1 KINGS 11:4

God is a jealous God who will not have His people worship any other god but Him.

He called Israel to wipe out entire nations that were spiritually perverted; nations given to idolatry, idol worship, sorcery, divination, occult involvement, witchcraft, human sacrifice, etc. All these are an abomination before God. These practices do not only affect individual bloodlines, they could affect entire nations. God warned Israel of such practices:

> And God spoke all these words: "I am the LORD your God, who brought you out of Egypt, out of the land of slavery. You shall

have no other gods before me. You shall not make for yourself an image in the form of anything in heaven above or on the earth beneath or in the waters below. You shall not bow down to them or worship them; for I, the LORD your God, am a jealous God, punishing the children for the sin of the parents to the third and fourth generation of those who hate me, but showing love to a thousand generations of those who love me and keep my commandments."

—EXODUS 20:1–6, NIV

An entire nation comes under reproach because of these things: "Righteousness exalteth a nation: but sin is a reproach to any people" (Prov. 14:34). The opposite is true of nations who seek the Lord: "Blessed is the nation whose God is the LORD; and the people whom he hath chosen for his own inheritance" (Ps. 33:12).

Let's look at some bloodlines that came under divine judgment and curses for their involvement in these practices.

Jeroboam

Jeroboam rebelled against Rehoboam the son of Solomon. He managed to gather some following and eventually divide the united kingdom of Israel into two—Northern Kingdom and Southern Kingdom. In the process of time, Satan captured his heart.

> And Jeroboam said in his heart, now shall the kingdom return to the house of David. If this people go up to do sacrifice in the house of the LORD at Jerusalem, then shall the heart of this people turn again unto their lord, even unto Rehoboam king of Judah, and they shall kill me, and go again to Rehoboam king of Judah. Whereupon the king took counsel, and made two calves of gold, and said unto them, It is too much for you to go up to Jerusalem: behold thy gods, O Israel, which brought thee up out of the land of Egypt.
>
> —1 KINGS 12:26–28

This act immediately brought divine curses upon him and his bloodline.

> Go, tell Jeroboam that this is what the LORD, the God of Israel, says: "I raised you up from among the people and appointed you

ruler over my people Israel. I tore the kingdom away from the house of David and gave it to you, but you have not been like my servant David, who kept my commands and followed me with all his heart, doing only what was right in my eyes. You have done more evil than all who lived before you. You have made for yourself other gods, idols made of metal; you have aroused my anger and turned your back on me. Because of this, I am going to bring disaster on the house of Jeroboam. I will cut off from Jeroboam every last male in Israel—slave or free. I will burn up the house of Jeroboam as one burns dung, until it is all gone. Dogs will eat those belonging to Jeroboam who die in the city, and the birds will feed on those who die in the country. The LORD has spoken!" As for you, go back home. When you set foot in your city, the boy will die. All Israel will mourn for him and bury him. He is the only one belonging to Jeroboam who will be buried, because he is the only one in the house of Jeroboam in whom the LORD, the God of Israel, has found anything good. The LORD will raise up for himself a king over Israel who will cut off the family of Jeroboam. Even now this is beginning to happen."

—1 KINGS 14:7–14, NIV

These prophesies were later fulfilled in the next chapter, in the days of the next generation. His descendants were carried into captivity and King Baasha made sure there was none left to continue the bloodline of Jeroboam.

Now the rest of the acts of Rehoboam, and all that he did, are they not written in the book of the chronicles of the kings of Judah? And there was war between Rehoboam and Jeroboam all their days.

—1 KINGS 14:29–30

King Saul

The family of Saul, first king of Israel, suffered because of the involvement of the old warrior in divination.

Then said Saul unto his servants, Seek me a woman that hath a familiar spirit that I may go to her, and enquire of her. And his servants said to him, Behold, there is a woman that hath a familiar spirit at Endor. And Saul disguised himself, and put on

other raiment, and he went, and two men with him, and they
came to the woman by night: and he said, I pray thee, divine
unto me by the familiar spirit, and bring me him up, whom I
shall name unto thee.

1 SAMUEL 28:7–8

When Saul first ascended to the throne, he did that which was right
in the sight of the Lord. He rid the land of those who practiced witchcraft and divination and God blessed him.

And the woman said unto him, Behold, thou knowest what Saul
hath done, how he hath cut off those that have familiar spirits,
and the wizards, out of the land: wherefore then layest thou a
snare for my life, to cause me to die?

—1 SAMUEL 28:9

In his later years, disobedience caused him to lose God's favor.

And Samuel said, Hath the LORD as great delight in burnt offerings and sacrifices, as in obeying the voice of the LORD? Behold,
to obey is better than sacrifice, and to hearken than the fat of
rams.

—1 SAMUEL 15:22

The Bible records Saul's sad and tragic end. He visited the witch of
Endor to dabble in witchcraft and familiar spirits. He also went into
the bedchamber (bedroom) of the witch, sat on her bed to eat food
(cooked by the witch), then rose and went into battle where he and the
next generation (his son Jonathan) were killed.

And the woman said unto him, Behold, thou knowest what Saul
hath done, how he hath cut off those that have familiar spirits, and
the wizards, out of the land: wherefore then layest thou a snare for
my life, to cause me to die? And Saul sware to her by the LORD,
saying, As the LORD liveth, there shall no punishment happen to
thee for this thing. Then said the woman, whom shall I bring up
unto thee? And he said, Bring me up Samuel...And the woman
had a fat calf in the house; and she hasted, and killed it, and took
flour, and kneaded it, and did bake unleavened bread thereof: And

she brought it before Saul, and before his servants; and they did
eat. Then they rose up, and went away that night.

—1 SAMUEL 28:9–11, 24–25

This story is condensed for the purposes of our studies; please refer to entire story in the Bible for detailed understanding. The only person left of his bloodline was Mephibosheth, Jonathan's son who was crippled in both legs and ended up living in Lodebar, a town of forgotten people.

And the king said, Is there not yet any of the house of Saul, that I may shew the kindness of God unto him? And Ziba said unto the king, Jonathan hath yet a son, which is lame on his feet. And the king said unto him, Where is he? And Ziba said unto the king, Behold, he is in the house of Machir, the son of Ammiel, in Lodebar.

—2 SAMUEL 9:3–4

King Solomon later wrote:

There is an evil which I have seen under the sun, as an error which proceedeth from the ruler: Folly is set in great dignity, and the rich sit in low place. I have seen servants upon horses, and princes walking as servants upon the earth.

—ECCLESIASTES 10:5–7

Saul committed folly in high places, an error and evil under the sun, and it affected his whole bloodline.

Child of God, it's time to take back what the devil stole from you! You have kingdom authority to command every devil, every curse and beggar or servant to get off your horse.

Ahab and Jezebel

The introduction of Ahab in scripture can send chills down anybody's spine.

And Ahab the son of Omri did evil in the sight of the LORD above all that were before him. And it came to pass, as if it had been a light thing for him to walk in the sins of Jeroboam the son of Nebat, that he took to wife Jezebel the daughter of Ethbaal king

of the Zidonians, and went and served Baal, and worshipped him.
And he reared up an altar for Baal in the house of Baal, which he
had built in Samaria. And Ahab made a grove; and Ahab did more
to provoke the LORD God of Israel to anger than all the kings of
Israel that were before him.

—1 KINGS 16:30–33

Verse 34 of 1 Kings 16 is a fulfillment of the prophetic declaration
of Joshua, the son of Nun. After the conquest of Jericho, Joshua pronounced this curse:

And Joshua adjured them at that time, saying, Cursed be the man
before the LORD, that riseth up and buildeth this city Jericho:
he shall lay the foundation thereof in his firstborn, and in his
youngest son shall he set up the gates of it.

—JOSHUA 6:26

Remember that a curse without a cause shall not stand: "So the
curse causeless shall not come" (Prov. 26:2b). Ahab blatantly ignored
the curse and permitted the walls to be rebuilt on his watch, thus the
curse was fulfilled.

In his days did Hiel the Bethelite build Jericho: he laid the foundation thereof in Abiram his firstborn, and set up the gates
thereof in his youngest son Segub, according to the word of the
LORD, which he spake by Joshua the son of Nun.

—1 KINGS 16:34

Together the dynamic evil duo, Ahab and Jezebel, engaged in the
total package of evil, shedding the innocent blood of Naboth and his
children and then forcefully taking possession of his vineyard which
was forbidden by law in Israel.

And it came to pass after these things, that Naboth the Jezreelite
had a vineyard, which was in Jezreel, hard by the palace of Ahab
king of Samaria...And the men of his city, even the elders and
the nobles who were the inhabitants in his city, did as Jezebel
had sent unto them, and as it was written in the letters which
she had sent unto them. They proclaimed a fast, and set Naboth
on high among the people. And there came in two men, children

of Belial, and sat before him: and the men of Belial witnessed against him, even against Naboth, in the presence of the people, saying, Naboth did blaspheme God and the king. Then they carried him forth out of the city, and stoned him with stones, that he died. Then they sent to Jezebel, saying, Naboth is stoned, and is dead. And it came to pass, when Jezebel heard that Naboth was stoned, and was dead, that Jezebel said to Ahab, Arise, take possession of the vineyard of Naboth the Jezreelite, which he refused to give thee for money: for Naboth is not alive, but dead.

—1 KINGS 21:1, 11–15

They engaged in witchcraft, sorcery, divination, spiritism, the occult, idolatry, and much more. Elijah the Tishbite pronounced judgment upon the house of Ahab in 1 Kings 21:19–24. Jehu, the son of Jehoshaphat, executed the judgment pronounced upon the house of Ahab and his entire bloodline.

And it came to pass, when Joram saw Jehu, that he said, Is it peace, Jehu? And he answered, What peace, so long as the whoredoms of thy mother Jezebel and her witchcrafts are so many? And Joram turned his hands, and fled, and said to Ahaziah, There is treachery, O Ahaziah. And Jehu drew a bow with his full strength, and smote Jehoram between his arms, and the arrow went out at his heart, and he sunk down in his chariot. Then said Jehu to Bidkar his captain, Take up, and cast him in the portion of the field of Naboth the Jezreelite: for remember how that, when I and thou rode together after Ahab his father, the LORD laid this burden upon him.

—2 KINGS 9:22–25

And when Jehu was come to Jezreel, Jezebel heard of it; and she painted her face, and tired her head, and looked out at a window. And as Jehu entered in at the gate, she said, had Zimri peace, who slew his master? And he lifted up his face to the window, and said, Who is on my side? Who? And there looked out to him two or three eunuchs. And he said, Throw her down. So they threw her down: and some of her blood was sprinkled on the wall, and on the horses: and he trode her under foot. And when he was come in, he did eat and drink, and said, Go, see now this cursed woman, and bury her: for she is a king's daughter. And they went to bury her: but they found no more of her than the skull, and the feet, and the palms of her hands. Wherefore they came again, and told him. And he said, This is the word of the LORD, which he spake by his servant Elijah the Tishbite, saying, In the portion of Jezreel shall dogs eat the flesh of Jezebel: And the carcass of Jezebel shall be as dung upon the face of the field in the portion of Jezreel; so that they shall not say, This is Jezebel.

—2 KINGS 9:30–37

The curse of Ahab passed on to his children and devoured them all.

Then he [Jehu] wrote a letter the second time to them, saying, If ye be mine, and if ye will hearken unto my voice, take ye the heads of the men your master's sons, and come to me to Jezreel by tomorrow this time. Now the king's sons, being seventy persons, were with the great men of the city, which brought them up. And it came to pass, when the letter came to them, that they took the king's sons, and slew seventy persons, and put their heads in baskets, and sent him them to Jezreel.

—2 KINGS 10:6–7

Ahab and all his sons suffered very violent deaths, but they had done worse to others. What an unfortunate end to a dynasty: "Evil shall slay the wicked" (Ps. 34:21a).

It is not too late to repent. There comes a time when even repentance can and may be too late. This is your hour! This is your time! This is your moment!

While it is said, To day if ye will hear his voice, harden not your hearts, as in the provocation.

—HEBREWS 3:15

I appeal to you therefore, brethren, and beg of you in view of [all] the mercies of God, to make a decisive dedication of your bodies [presenting all your members and faculties] as a living sacrifice, holy (devoted, consecrated) and well pleasing to God, which is your reasonable (rational, intelligent) service and spiritual worship.
[ROMANS 12:1, AMP]

Chapter 12
SEXUAL DOORWAYS

FORNICATION AND ADULTERY

GOD IS A holy God and He expects His children to be holy. The apostle Paul admonished the church of Corinth to keep their vessel (body) clean because, not only is it the temple of the Holy Spirit, but also we are also joined with the Lord and have become one with Him.

> Do you not know that your bodies are members of Christ himself? Shall I then take the members of Christ and unite them with a prostitute? Never! Do you not know that he who unites himself with a prostitute is one with her in body? For it is said, "The two will become one flesh." But whoever is united with the Lord is one with him in spirit. Flee from sexual immorality. All other sins a person commits are outside the body, but whoever sins sexually, sins against their own body. Do you not know that your bodies are temples of the Holy Spirit, who is in you, whom you have received from God? You are not your own.
>
> —1 CORINTHIANS 6:15–19, NIV

Under the old covenant, the presence of God dwelt in the ark of the covenant. The ark has been replaced under the new covenant by our bodies and therefore must constantly be under the purifying flow of the blood of the eternal covenant. It must be presented daily as a living sacrifice unto the Lord.

> I beseech you therefore, brethren, by the mercies of God, that ye present your bodies a living sacrifice, holy, acceptable unto God, which is your reasonable service.
>
> —ROMANS 12:1

Fornication and adultery should not even be mentioned among believers. The Bible teaches that it is an act of disobedience and the wrath of God comes upon those who engage in this act.

> But fornication, and all uncleanness, or covetousness, let it not be once named among you, as becometh saints; Neither filthiness, nor foolish talking, nor jesting, which are not convenient: but rather giving of thanks. For this ye know, that no whoremonger, nor unclean person, nor covetous man, who is an idolater, hath any inheritance in the kingdom of Christ and of God. Let no man deceive you with vain words: for because of these things cometh the wrath of God upon the children of disobedience.
>
> —EPHESIANS 5:3–6

Seduction of Israel

When Balaam failed in his quest to curse Israel, he advised Balak how to bring down the wrath of God to destroy His covenant children. Balaam encouraged Balak to seduce Israel into sexual sins. The kings of Moab and Midian acted upon the demonically-inspired advice of Balaam. They organized a big feast in honor of their gods and invited the children of Israel to participate in the celebrations. Israel fell into this trap and went into great apostasy bringing down the wrath of the Holy One of Israel to destroy them. Zimri, a prince of the tribe of Simeon, was not ashamed to let his people witness his loose moral and evil conduct.

Apostle Paul told us in 1 Corinthians 10:8: "Neither let us commit fornication, as some of them committed, and fell in one day three and twenty thousand." Twenty three thousand men died, in addition to the one thousand leaders who were also killed and hung.

> While Israel was staying in Shittim, the men began to indulge in sexual immorality with Moabite women, who invited them to the sacrifices to their gods. The people ate the sacrificial meal and bowed down before these gods. So Israel yoked themselves to the Baal of Peor. And the Lord's anger burned against them. The LORD said to Moses, "Take all the leaders of these people, kill them and expose them in broad daylight before the Lord, so that the Lord's fierce anger may turn away from Israel."...Those who died in the plague numbered 24,000.
>
> —NUMBERS 25:1–4, 9, NIV

The children of Israel strayed from obeying the Lord completely and "wandered off to follow the way of Balaam son of Bezer, who loved the wages of wickedness" (2 Pet. 2:15, NIV). Balaam was "rebuked for his wrongdoing by his donkey—an animal without speech—who spoke with a human voice and restrained the prophet's madness" (v. 16, NIV). Balaam's donkey saw the angel of the Lord with a sword drawn against Balaam and refused to go forward. But Balaam was so consumed and blinded by his greed and self-righteousness that he could not discern what was happening, so he kept hitting the beast until it spoke and rebuked him.

Could this have been God's grace extended to him to spare his life and to give him a second chance to get back on track? This same grace is being extended to you now; don't procrastinate much longer in obeying the still small voice of the Holy Ghost to do the right thing. "These people are springs without water and mists driven by a storm. Blackest darkness is reserved for them" (2 Pet. 2:17, NIV).

Besides innumerable sexual transmitted diseases, engaging in fornication and adultery reduces the believer to "springs without water and mists driven along before a tempest" (2 Pet. 2:17, AMP). Demonic spirits could also be contacted through the act of sexual promiscuity.

If you have a sexual encounter with one that is possessed by demons, the two of you become one spirit. Simply put, you contact those spirits, share in those spirits, and receive the curse that follows that individual. Their curse becomes your curse also. Jesus warned us regarding the curse of Balaam:

> But I have a few things against thee, because thou hast there them that hold the doctrine of Balaam, who taught Balac to cast a stumbling block before the children of Israel, to eat things sacrificed unto idols, and to commit fornication.
>
> —REVELATION 2:14

How terrible to have known the love of Christ and His saving grace but now, you have become one with someone sold out completely to the evil one through sex!

Moses also described the curse of Balaam:

Behold, these caused the children of Israel, through the counsel
of Balaam, to commit trespass against the Lord in the matter
of Peor, and there was a plague among the congregation of the
Lord. Now therefore kill every male among the little ones, and
kill every woman that hath known man by lying with him.

—Numbers 31:16–17

*Please, child of God, don't allow a few minutes of pleasure to launch
you into a lifetime of regrets. Let your life be precious in your own eyes
and those of your loved ones and ultimately in the sight of God.*

Soul Ties

If sexual promiscuity is not broken and properly dealt with to free the
believer from its stronghold, one can slip into soul ties, even though
they have moved on in life. There will always be that constant pull
and desire for the person with whom you had the encounter. This
overpowering desire and constant pull is called a soul tie. The negative effect of a soul tie always benefits the devil because it feeds his
agenda when two people know each other sexually outside of marriage. Their bodies, souls, and spirits become one and are defiled.
Dinah, the daughter of Leah whom she bore to Jacob, was defiled by
Shechem, son of Hamor the Hivite.

Dinah and the Shechemites

Now Dinah, the daughter Leah had borne to Jacob, went out to
visit the women of the land. When Shechem son of Hamor the
Hivite, the ruler of that area, saw her, he took her and raped
her. His heart was drawn to Dinah daughter of Jacob; he loved
the young woman and spoke tenderly to her…And Hamor com-
muned with them saying, the soul of my son Shechem longeth for
your daughter: I pray you give her him to wife.

—Genesis 34:1–3, 8, niv

The scripture confirms that Shechem did not truly love Dinah, but
rather, there was a soul tie.

> And the Babylonians came to her into the bed of love, and they
> defiled her with their whoredom, and she was polluted with
> them, and her mind was alienated from them.
>
> —EZEKIEL 23:17

Dinah was defiled, but God by His divine wisdom used this incident to bring this heathen nation into covenant with Himself. God can turn your mistakes into victories if you let Him. Don't let adultery or fornication ruin your life.

> But whoso committeth adultery with a woman lacketh understanding: he that doeth it destroyeth his own soul.
>
> —PROVERBS 6:32

Please clean your vessel through the cleansing blood of Jesus and commit to the Word and prayer. Escape any further bondage or curse into which this may bury you. It is never too late to reach out to God and call upon Him for help, for He *will* deliver you.

> Drink waters out of thine own cistern, and running waters out of
> thine own well. Let thy fountains be dispersed abroad, and rivers
> of waters in the streets. Let them be only thine own, and not
> strangers' with thee. Let thy fountain be blessed: and rejoice with
> the wife of thy youth. Let her be as the loving hind and pleasant
> roe; let her breasts satisfy thee at all times; and be thou ravished
> always with her love.
>
> —PROVERBS 5:15–19

The Genesis account of marriage is very clear about a man cleaving unto his wife.

> Therefore shall a man leave his father and his mother, and shall
> cleave unto his wife: and they shall be one flesh.
>
> —GENESIS 2:24

The word *cleave* is defined as to stick or hold together and resist separation; it also means adhere, cling, and cohere.[1] To separate the two joined together requires external force to split, cut, tear, break, amputate, butcher, chop, etc. Two souls are tied together in marriage, and this covenant is not meant to be broken. Jesus said, "What therefore God hath joined together, let not man put asunder" (Mark 10:9).

To divide is to rip the joined souls apart. This is the reason divorce is always painful and oftentimes very messy and ugly, tearing children apart and destroying their hopes for future relationships. Every time your share your cistern with someone, other than your spouse, you are joined as one and the soul tie could become a stronghold constantly pulling on you to have lustful desires for that person, You have sinned against your body.

> What? know ye not that he which is joined to a harlot is one body? for two, saith he, shall be one flesh...Flee fornication. Every sin that a man doeth is without the body; but he that committeth fornication sinneth against his own body.
>
> —1 CORINTHIANS 6:16, 18

And you have also defiled your marital bed.

> Marriage is honourable in all, and the bed undefiled: but whoremongers and adulterers God will judge.
>
> —HEBREWS 13:4

So if the Son sets you free, you will be free indeed.

> —JOHN 8:36, NIV

You are snared with the words of your lips, you are
caught by the speech of your mouth.
[Proverbs 6:2, amp]

Chapter 13
DESTRUCTIVE WORDS

MANY BELIEVERS HAVE destroyed their destinies and those of the next generation through uncontrolled words released carelessly. Jesus warned us in the Gospels;

> But I say unto you, That every idle word that men shall speak, they shall give account thereof in the day of judgment. For by thy words thou shalt be justified, and by thy words thou shalt be condemned.
>
> —MATTHEW 12:36–37

Destructive words are sometimes spoken carelessly and harshly during moments of hurt, anger, argument, bitterness, jealousy, and envy. This can also happen when seeking revenge, when feeling unappreciated, or even in moments of casual conversation. Some people let loose innocently without premeditation or processing the words in their minds. They defend themselves by saying, "This is who I am; take it or leave it."

Wisdom, spoken of in Proverbs, does not do this:

> Hear; for I will speak of excellent things; and the opening of my lips shall be right things. For my mouth shall speak truth; and wickedness is an abomination to my lips. All the words of my mouth are in righteousness; there is nothing forward or perverse in them.
>
> —PROVERBS 8:6–8

Solomon warned us of the consequences of such carless words and their potency to do harm.

> A man's belly shall be satisfied with the fruit of his mouth; and with the increase of his lips shall he be filled. Death and life are

in the power of the tongue: and they that love it shall eat the fruit thereof.

—PROVERBS 18:20–21

Thou art snared with the words of thy mouth, thou art taken with the words of thy mouth.

—PROVERBS 6:2

A young lady came to see me to agree with her for a job she was seeking. After much fasting and prayer, favor was released and she found a very lucrative job with very good benefits. A few months later, she came back to see me and she said, "Pastor, you are a praying man and I notice when you pray things happen." She said, "Would you pray with me for another job?" I asked her, "What about your current job?" She responded, "I don't work for that company anymore." She said, "I told my supervisor my mind and reminded her that this is America and we have freedom of speech." Many people like this woman have talked themselves out of their blessings and backed themselves up into a corner. The book of remembrance in Malachi 3:16 records the conversations of the saints.

> "You have spoken arrogantly against me," says the LORD. "Yet you ask, 'What have we said against you?' You have said, 'It is futile to serve God. What do we gain by carrying out his requirements and going about like mourners before the LORD Almighty? But now we call the arrogant blessed. Certainly evildoers prosper, and even when they put God to the test, they get away with it.'" Then those who feared the LORD talked with each other, and the LORD listened and heard. A scroll of remembrance was written in his presence concerning those who feared the LORD and honored his name. "On the day when I act," says the LORD Almighty, "they will be my treasured possession. I will spare them, just as a father has compassion and spares his son who serves him.
>
> —MALACHI 3:13–17, NIV

Rebecca

Isaac, second generation in the bloodline of Abraham, was old and blind. He wanted to pronounce a benediction over his oldest son, Esau. Rebecca, his wife, preferred Jacob, the younger brother, over Esau. This was probably based on the word of the Lord when she took seed of the twin brothers (Gen. 25:23). She persuaded Jacob to deceive his father to obtain the blessing. Jacob said to his mom, "My father peradventure will feel me, and I shall seem to him as a deceiver; and I shall bring a curse upon me, and not a blessing" (Gen. 27:12). Rebecca responded back with these destructive words: "Upon me be thy curse, my son: only obey my voice, and go fetch me them" (v. 13).

Wow! What a mess! By high-level conspiracy and deception, she succeeded in getting the blessing for Jacob. Shortly after, for fear of what Esau planned to do to Jacob, she advised him to escape to Laban until Esau was appeased. She never again laid eyes on Jacob her beloved. Telephones were not available in those days, which also meant she never heard his voice again before dying. Read of the sad confession she made to the blind old husband who was near death and could not comfort her in any form or shape.

> Then Rebekah said to Isaac, "I'm disgusted with living because of these Hittite women. If Jacob takes a wife from among the women of this land, from Hittite women like these, my life will not be worth living."
>
> —GENESIS 27:46, NIV

What a miserable way for the daughter-in-law of the old general and patriarch Abraham to go out. Let the Love of Christ constrain you to articulate and process your words with the wisdom of God within you.

> For the love of Christ constraineth us; because we thus judge, that if one died for all, then were all dead: And that he died for all, that they which live should not henceforth live unto themselves, but unto him which died for them, and rose again.
>
> —2 CORINTHIANS 5:14–15

Tale of two cities

During the Passion of the Christ, the Jews used their words to invoke curses upon themselves and subsequent generations. Their story is the tale of two cities.

> "What shall I do, then, with Jesus who is called the Messiah?" Pilate asked. They all answered, "Crucify him!" "Why? What crime has he committed?" asked Pilate. But they shouted all the louder,

"Crucify him!" When Pilate saw that he was getting nowhere, but that instead an uproar was starting, he took water and washed his hands in front of the crowd. "I am innocent of this man's blood," he said. "It is your responsibility!" All the people answered, "His blood is on us and on our children!"

—MATTHEW 27:22–25, NIV

Rome, represented by Pilate, knew the consequences of innocent blood. Pilate's wife had warned him of her dream.

He knew it was out of self-interest that they had handed Jesus over to him. While Pilate was sitting on the judge's seat, his wife sent him this message: "Don't have anything to do with that innocent man, for I have suffered a great deal today in a dream because of him."

—MATTHEW 27:19, NIV

Then all the elders of the town nearest the body shall wash their hands over the heifer whose neck was broken in the valley, and they shall declare: "Our hands did not shed this blood, nor did our eyes see it done. Accept this atonement for your people Israel, whom you have redeemed, LORD, and do not hold your people guilty of the blood of an innocent person." Then the bloodshed will be atoned for, and you will have purged from yourselves the guilt of shedding innocent blood, since you have done what is right in the eyes of the LORD.

—DEUTERONOMY 21:6–9, NIV

The Jews, represented by the elders, did the unthinkable. While Pilate washed his hands off the shedding of the royal blood of the eternal covenant, they, by their choice, accepted the curses upon themselves and their children. The women were outside the gates during the trials, for that was the custom of the day. They were crying for the Messiah who had fed them, healed their children, spoken words of life to them, and comforted them. They would later find out the careless and destructive words of their husbands in the judgment court of Pilate, as the gates were opened and Jesus, bloodied from the beating at the whipping post, walked past them under the weight of the cross. He spoke these words:

Jesus turned and said to them, "Daughters of Jerusalem, do not weep for me; weep for yourselves and for your children. For the time will come when you will say, 'Blessed are the childless women, the wombs that never bore and the breasts that never nursed!' Then they will say to the mountains, 'Fall on us!' and to the hills, 'Cover us!' For if people do these things when the tree is green, what will happen when it is dry?" Two other men, both criminals, were also led out with him to be executed.

—LUKE 23:28–32, NIV

These words proved to be true in AD 70 when General Titus destroyed Jerusalem and killed men and women. The destroyers opened up pregnant women and crushed their babies upon the walls and sold others into slavery, according to Josephus, a Jewish historian.[1]

Jesus was and is the green tree in the above scripture, but the Jews preferred a dry tree.

He came unto his own, and his own received him not.

—JOHN 1:11

I am come in my Father's name, and ye receive me not: if another shall come in his own name, him ye will receive.

—JOHN 5:43

PLEASE WATCH YOUR WORDS

A lady called me one day hoping to get sympathy and support from me about a situation going on in their church based on a decision the founder made. I immediately stopped her before she could put a full sentence together. I advised her to break ranks with anybody taking sides against the leader and to go before God in repentance. I gave her several scriptures including the story I'm about to share with you from the Bible.

David had issues with his rebellious son Absalom. As a father who loved his family, David did what he felt was best at the time to prevent engaging Absalom in direct confrontation. By wisdom he left the palace until the problem was resolved. Shimei, from Saul's clan, took advantage of this situation to express his dislike for the king. He harbored bitterness and hatred in his heart towards David because he blamed David for the downfall of King Saul. Shimei picked the wrong battle and was careless with his words.

> As King David approached Bahurim, a man from the same clan as Saul's family came out from there. His name was Shimei son of Gera, and he cursed as he came out. He pelted David and all the king's officials with stones, though all the troops and the special guard were on David's right and left. As he cursed, Shimei said, "Get out, get out, you murderer, you scoundrel! The LORD has repaid you for all the blood you shed in the household of Saul, in whose place you have reigned. The LORD has given the kingdom into the hands of your son Absalom. You have come to ruin because you are a murderer!"
>
> —2 SAMUEL 16:5–8, NIV

Those words would come back to haunt him like a plague. For it is written,

> He suffered no man to do them wrong: yea, he reproved kings for their sakes; Saying, Touch not mine anointed, and do my prophets no harm.
>
> —PSALM 105:14–15

> Thou art snared with the words of thy mouth, thou art taken with the words of thy mouth.
>
> —PROVERBS 6:2

> He that hath no rule over his own spirit is like a city that is broken down, and without walls.
>
> —PROVERBS 25:28

> In the multitude of words there wanteth not sin: but he that refraineth his lips is wise.
>
> —PROVERBS 10:19

Shimei signed his own death warrant through idle destructive words.

> The king also said to Shimei, "You know in your heart all the wrong you did to my father David. Now the LORD will repay you for your wrongdoing. But King Solomon will be blessed, and David's throne will remain secure before the LORD forever." Then

the king gave the order to Benaiah son of Jehoiada, and he went out and struck Shimei down and he died. The kingdom was now established in Solomon's hands.

—1 Kings 2:44–46, niv

After the death of Saul, David in his lamentation, warned the children of Israel about the dangers of lifting their tongue against the anointed of God under any circumstance. He warned that it gives an occasion to the ungodly to rejoice and triumph.

The beauty of Israel is slain upon thy high places: how are the mighty fallen! Tell it not in Gath, publish it not in the streets of Askelon; lest the daughters of the Philistines rejoice, lest the daughters of the uncircumcised triumph.

—2 Samuel 1:19–20

From today I see you blessing yourself and your household with your words. I see you blessing your surroundings and your bloodline in the name of Jesus Christ.

These six things the Lord hates, indeed, seven are an abomination to Him:
A proud look [the spirit that makes one overestimate himself and under-
estimate others], a lying tongue, and hands that shed innocent blood
[PROVERBS 6:16–17, AMP]

Chapter 14

SHEDDING INNOCENT BLOOD

PROVERBS 6 CONTAINS a list of abominable things that God detests, including hands that shed innocent blood. King James says it this way:

> These six things doth the LORD hate: yea, seven are an abomination unto him: A proud look, a lying tongue, and hands that shed innocent blood.
>
> —PROVERBS 6:15–17

The first person to shed innocent blood was Cain.

> And Cain talked with Abel his brother: and it came to pass, when they were in the field, that Cain rose up against Abel his brother, and slew him.
>
> —GENESIS 4:8

He spilled the blood of Abel and incurred the curse of the vagabond. He became a fugitive in the face of the earth. The blood of Abel began to cry against Cain.

> The LORD said, "What have you done? Listen! Your brother's blood cries out to me from the ground. Now you are under a curse and driven from the ground, which opened its mouth to receive your brother's blood from your hand. When you work the ground, it will no longer yield its crops for you. You will be a restless wanderer on the earth."
>
> —GENESIS 4:10–12, NIV

The posterity of Abel was cut off forever by his death. In murder one not only sins against God and the man he kills but also against the murdered man's posterity for eternal generations.

Another one of Cain's descendants became the first polygamist and secondly a murderer. He claims to have killed in self-defense.

> And Lamech took unto him two wives: the name of the one was
> Adah, and the name of the other Zillah…And Lamech said unto
> his wives, Adah and Zillah, Hear my voice; ye wives of Lamech,
> hearken unto my speech: for I have slain a man to my wounding,
> and a young man to my hurt.
> —GENESIS 4:19, 23

Cain himself became the first mayor of the first city called Enoch
and increased in wickedness.

> Not as Cain, who was of that wicked one, and slew his brother.
> And wherefore slew he him? Because his own works were evil,
> and his brother's righteous.
> —1 JOHN 3:12

> Woe unto them! for they have gone in the way of Cain, and ran
> greedily after the error of Balaam for reward, and perished in the
> gainsaying of Core.
> —JUDE 1:11

Cain's descendants cared nothing about God. Seth came on the
scene and produced his bloodline. Then men began to call upon the
name of the Lord.

> And to Seth, to him also there was born a son; and he called his
> name Enos: then began men to call upon the name of the LORD.
> —GENESIS 4:26

Cain's bloodline was completely wiped out in the flood of Noah.

> And, behold, I, even I, do bring a flood of waters upon the earth, to
> destroy all flesh, wherein is the breath of life, from under heaven;
> and everything that is in the earth shall die. But with thee will I
> establish my covenant; and thou shalt come into the ark, thou, and
> thy sons, and thy wife, and thy sons' wives with thee.
> —GENESIS 6:17–18

> God judgeth the righteous, and God is angry with the wicked
> every day.
> —PSALM 7:11

Shedding innocent blood is also tampering with God's plan and purpose for the murdered victim. This individual could possibly be a potential lawyer, doctor, pastor, prophet, president, or even the deliverer of his people.

THE PHARAOH WHO KNEW NOT JOSEPH

In Exodus 1:8 we read of a Pharaoh who arose who did not know Joseph. This king began to shed innocent blood by sacrificing every male Hebrew child to the Nile god.

> And Pharaoh charged his people saying, Every son that is born ye shall cast into the river, and every daughter ye shall save alive.
>
> —EXODUS 1:22

His target was the deliverer, but God's plan is always superior. Moses was delivered from the gods of the Nile. The Egyptians considered the Nile to be the father of the gods and the father of life. During the Exodus from Egypt, God visited divine judgment on every firstborn of Egypt.

> And it came to pass that at midnight the LORD smote all the first born in Egypt, from the firstborn of Pharaoh that sat on his throne unto the firstborn of the captive that was in the dungeon and all the firstborn of cattle.
>
> —EXODUS 12:29

He also destroyed Pharaoh's army in the Red Sea.

> And Moses stretched his hand over the sea, and the sea returned to his strength when the morning appeared; and the Egyptians fled against it; and the Lord overthrew the Egyptians in the midst of the sea. And the waters returned, and covered the chariots, and the horsemen, and all the host of Pharaoh that came into the sea after them; there remained not so much as one of them.
>
> —EXODUS 14:27–28

You reap what you sow. I guess one could say, as Mark Anthony said to the Roman citizens in his speech at the burial of Caesar, "The evil that men do lives after them."[2] The economy of Egypt also went bankrupt in one day. God hates hands that shed innocent blood.

These six things doth the LORD hate: yea, seven are an abomination unto him: A proud look, a lying tongue, and hands that shed
innocent blood.

—PROVERBS 6:16–17

There is always a price to pay for shedding innocent blood. The price for
shedding innocent blood can be very detrimental. Some have shed innocent blood through hit-and-run vehicle accidents, hatred and revenge,
insurance greed, drug wars, abortions, etc. However this occurred, each
must take personal responsibility for their actions. Take the proper steps
to write the wrong, repent before the Lord sincerely, and fall upon His
mercy; for His mercies are so great.

And David said unto Gad, I am in a great strait: let me fall now
into the hand of the LORD; for very great are his mercies: but let
me not fall into the hand of man.

—1 CHRONICLES 21:13

For as the heaven is high above the earth, so great is his mercy
toward them that fear him.

—PSALM 103:11

JUDAS AND THE INNOCENT BLOOD OF JESUS

Judas Iscariot was handpicked by Jesus as one of His original twelve
disciples (see Matthew 10:1–4). He was called an apostle and a bishop
(see Acts 1:20). He witnessed and experienced the great wonders of
God in the ministry of Jesus. In fact, he was given authority to heal
the sick and to set the captives free and he was the treasurer of the
group. He later turned out to be a thief. True to his nature, he allowed
Satan to enter his heart through offense and eventually betrayed his
Lord with the Judas kiss (Matt. 26:48).

Judas helped the blood-thirsty enemies of Jesus to shed royal innocent blood. In John 6:70 Jesus referred to him as a devil. Judas lost
everything, including eternal salvation. The combination of stealing,
greed, offense, disloyalty, betrayal, and ultimately shedding innocent blood took him to a place of eternal damnation; no true repentance was found in him. In Mark 14:21 Jesus warned, "The Son of Man
indeed goes just as it is written of Him, but woe to that man by whom

the Son of Man is betrayed! It would have been good for that man if he had never been born" (NKJV).

BLOODLINE OF HEROD

The Herods have a history of shedding innocent blood. Herod the Great, son of Antipater, started off doing good. He rebuilt the Jewish temple.

> Then said the Jews, Forty and six years was this temple in building, and wilt thou rear it up in three days?
>
> —JOHN 2:20

When he heard about the birth of the Messiah, who would be King, Satan entered Herod's heart and he ordered the slaughter of innocent children in his quest to get rid of the Deliverer.

> Then Herod, when he saw that he was mocked of the wise men, was exceeding wroth, and sent forth, and slew all the children that were in Bethlehem, and in all the coasts thereof, from two years old and under, according to the time which he had diligently enquired of the wise men.
>
> —MATTHEW 2:16

Herod died at an old age, but the harm had already been done. The kingdom was divided and the evil seed he had sown began to take root in his son. Herod Antipas succeeded his father and he also shed innocent blood, even though he reverenced John as a prophet and loved listening to his message while he was in prison.

> For Herod himself had given orders to have John arrested, and he had him bound and put in prison. He did this because of Herodias, his brother Philip's wife, whom he had married for John had been saying to Herod, "It is not lawful for you to have your brother's wife." So Herodias nursed a grudge against John and wanted to kill him. But she was not able to, because Herod feared John and protected him, knowing him to be a righteous and holy man. When Herod heard John, he was greatly puzzled; yet he liked to listen to him.
>
> —MARK 6:17–20, NIV

John's rebuke of Herod marrying Herodias, his brother Phillip's wife, did not sit well with him or the woman. At her mother's suggestion, the daughter of Herodias requested the head of John the Baptist. Herod Antipas handed it to her on a silver platter.

> The king was greatly distressed, but because of his oaths and his dinner guests, he did not want to refuse her. So he immediately sent an executioner with orders to bring John's head. The man went, beheaded John in the prison, and brought back his head on a platter. He presented it to the girl, and she gave it to her mother.
> —MARK 6:26–28, NIV

After killing the forerunner of Jesus, Herod Antipas turned his focus on the Messiah. When Jesus was arrested, Herod gathered his men and they stood Jesus in their midst and mocked Him.

> When Herod saw Jesus, he was greatly pleased, because for a long time he had been wanting to see him. From what he had heard about him, he hoped to see him perform a sign of some sort. He plied him with many questions, but Jesus gave him no answer. The chief priests and the teachers of the law were standing there, vehemently accusing him. Then Herod and his soldiers ridiculed and mocked him. Dressing him in an elegant robe, they sent him back to Pilate.
> —LUKE 23:8–11, NIV

Pilate, a heathen leader, attempted to set Jesus free. But Herod, by conspiracy, befriended Pilate and fed into Satan's plan to execute the Messiah. Herod Agrippa, the son of Aristobulus, grandson of Herod the Great, succeeded Antipas. He continued the family tradition of killing the prophets and shedding innocent blood.

> Now about that time Herod the king stretched forth his hands to vex certain of the church. And he killed James the brother of John with the sword.
> —ACTS 12:1–2

After James he arrested Peter and imprisoned him with the hope of killing him on the big day to gain popularity.

And because he saw it pleased the Jews, he proceeded further to take Peter also. (Then were the days of unleavened bread.) And when he had apprehended him, he put him in prison, and delivered him to four quaternion of soldiers to keep him; intending after Easter to bring him forth to the people.

—Acts 12:3–4

God intervened and set Peter free through the prayers of the saints.

Peter therefore was kept in prison: but prayer was made without ceasing of the church unto God for him. And when Herod would have brought him forth, the same night Peter was sleeping between two soldiers, bound with two chains: and the keepers before the door kept the prison. And, behold, the angel of the Lord came upon him, and a light shined in the prison: and he smote Peter on the side, and raised him up, saying, Arise up quickly. And his chains fell off from his hands.

—Acts 12:5–7

When his plan failed, Herod executed the prison keepers.

And when Herod had sought for him, and found him not, he examined the keepers, and commanded that they should be put to death. And he went down from Judaea to Caesarea, and there abode.

—Acts 12:19

Pride Goes before a Fall

Agrippa exalted himself above measure, and an angel of the Lord killed him publicly.

And upon a set day Herod, arrayed in royal apparel, sat upon his throne, and made an oration unto them. And the people gave a shout, saying, It is the voice of a god, and not of a man. And immediately the angel of the Lord smote him, because he gave not God the glory: and he was eaten of worms, and gave up the ghost.

—Acts 12:21–23

Agrippa II was the fourth generation of the Herod's bloodline which came into power. He had opportunity to repent and break the curse on his bloodline. The apostle Paul witnessed to him to no avail.

King Agrippa, believest thou the prophets? I know that thou
believest. Then Agrippa said unto Paul, Almost thou persuadest
me to be a Christian. And Paul said, I would to God, that not
only thou, but also all that hear me this day, were both almost,
and altogether such as I am, except these bonds.

—Acts 26:27–29

In verse 28, he admitted that the Apostle Paul almost converted him
within the short time of their encounter. Agrippa II actually joined
forces with General Titus in AD 70 to massacre his own people, shedding much innocent blood. This act fulfilled the prophecy of Jesus at
the gates of Delarosa. The Herods were Edomites, descendants of Esau,
half-brother of Jacob. Each generation experienced God's grace and
mercy and had the opportunity to break the iniquity and curse of the
previous generation, but they chose not to. Herod the Great could have
embraced baby Jesus, but he chose to kill. Herod Antipas could have
embraced the prophet John the Baptist, but he chose to cut off his head.
He later met Jesus Himself, but chose to make mockery of the Messiah
and later sent him to Pilate to be killed. Herod Agrippa chose to stretch
his hands against the church. He killed the apostle James and attempted
to kill apostle Peter. Herod Agrippa II, fourth generation, joined Titus
against his own people after turning deaf ears to the apostle Paul.

That same grace and mercy of God is extended to everyone reading
this book. Unlike the stubborn Herods, you can be the generation that
broke and stopped the curse of your bloodline.

Yes you can!

Fiji: The Repentance of a Cannibal Village

Fiji, once called "cannibal islands," cannibalism was widespread.
Australian Pastor Thomas Baker of London Missionary Society
arrived in Fiji in 1859…On July 21, 1867, the Rev. Thomas Baker
and eight Fijian of his followers were killed with the hatchet. "We
ate everything except boots," says a witness of the drama. This
act of cannibalism on this mission is the cause of a curse…of the
community Nabutautau. The village in the mountains inland from
the main island of the archipelago, Viti Levu, is deprived of the
lush vegetation dominant in the region, and its 120 inhabitants are
struggling to feed themselves. The village has neither a school nor

roads or medical equipment…Many family lines have disappeared, no child has been able to go beyond high school…"The other Fijians want us to be punished for what happened," said Tomasi Baravilala, a village elder…Years after this act of cannibalism, the descendants…lift the curse befallen their community by repenting of their past…They will ask forgiveness from the eleven descendants of Rev. Baker…Mr. Tomasi Baravilala launched, "Tell the world that we ask we receive forgiveness and perhaps more help…"

The ceremony opened with the ritual of kava, a traditional drink. Its high point was "breaking the chain of the curse," symbolized by a release of balloons made by the family of Thomas Baker. Youth of the village have also played a part…Together, they participated in a rite of reconciliation…The villagers have also returned to the family Bible Baker, his comb, and the soles of his boots. The President of Fiji, Laisenia Qarase (2000–2006), for his part described as [a] "beautiful act" the initiative of the villagers of Nabutautau.[1]

I have watched the documentary several times; and each time I saw it, it brought tears to my eyes. I am also reminded of the power of forgiveness and the efficacy of the precious blood of Jesus that breaks every curse and reverses the effects to release the blessing. As pastors came together to call upon the name of the Lord, they are not disappointed.

> For the scripture saith, Whosoever believeth on him shall not be ashamed. For there is no difference between the Jew and the Greek: for the same Lord over all is rich unto all that call upon him. For whosoever shall call upon the name of the Lord shall be saved.
> —ROMANS 10:11–13

Prisons were emptied out as hard-core prisoners and drug dealers were converted to Christ; many become preachers of the gospel. The land was healed and gave bumper crops. The waters were also healed as fishermen came home with unusual catch of very healthy fish of all manner. Fetish and native doctors gave up their practice and turned to the Lord for help. The prime minister elect signed the constitution of Fiji with red ink, dedicating it to the Lord. Fiji experienced a transformation that other nations desire and seek after. This is what happens when a people repent of the sins of their fathers and turn from their wicked ways: curses are broken and captivity turned around—just like we read in the Bible when Israel turned back to the God of their salvation.

> If my people, which are called by my name, shall humble themselves, and pray, and seek my face, and turn from their wicked ways; then will I hear from heaven, and will forgive their sin, and will heal their land.
>
> —2 CHRONICLES 7:14

The rich transformation of the island of Fiji can happen to any family, tribe, village, or nation. Salvation is the beginning of breaking and reversing any curse, and it is available to all.

> He came unto his own, and his own received him not. But as many as received him, to them gave he power to become the sons of God, even to them that believe on his name.
>
> —JOHN 1:11–12

> For God so loved the world, that he gave his only begotten Son, that whosoever believeth in him should not perish, but have everlasting life.
>
> —JOHN 3:16

> Righteousness exalteth a nation: but sin is a reproach to any people.
>
> —PROVERBS 14:34

> Blessed is the nation whose God is the LORD; and the people whom he hath chosen for his own inheritance.
>
> —PSALMS 33:12

Your family and bloodline is next in line to experience God's gift of salvation to break the curses and reverse their effects so you can begin to walk in the blessings.

> If ye be willing and obedient, ye shall eat the good of the land.
>
> —ISAIAH 1:19

PART II
THE REMEDY,
THE CURE:
JESUS, THE CURSE BREAKER

He personally bore our sins in His [own] body on the tree [as on an altar and offered Himself on it], that we might die (cease to exist) to sin and live to righteousness. By His wounds you have been healed.
[1 Peter 2:24, AMP]

Chapter 15
LET THE HEALING BEGIN

WE HAVE DISCUSSED various types of curses and their causes. Question now is, how do we break these curses in order to walk in the blessings of salvation?

The breaking of any curse begins with being born again—knowing and accepting Jesus as your personal Lord and Savior after repenting from every sin and receiving His free gift of salvation.

> For all have sinned, and come short of the glory of God.
> —ROMANS 3:23

The several benefits of salvation become available through the finished work of Christ on the cross. Seven hundred years before the birth of the Messiah, Isaiah prophesied and summed up His mission— a mission that redeemed the entire human race from the cataclysmic event that took place in the Garden of Eden to derail mankind, beginning with Adam. The cross where Jesus suffered and died became the place of divine exchange. Through the disobedience of the first Adam, mankind was alienated from God. But by the obedience of the second Adam, Jesus became the perfect sacrifice to satisfy a broken law, thereby reconciling us back to God.

> Forasmuch as ye know that ye were not redeemed with corruptible things, as silver and gold, from your vain conversation received by tradition from your fathers; But with the precious blood of Christ, as of a lamb without blemish and without spot: Who verily was foreordained before the foundation of the world, but was manifest in these last times for you.
> —1 PETER 1:18–20

Therefore, if anyone is in Christ, the new creation has come: The old has gone, the new is here! All this is from God, who reconciled us to himself through Christ and gave us the ministry of reconciliation: that God was reconciling the world to himself in Christ, not counting people's sins against them. And he has committed to us the message of reconciliation.

—2 CORINTHIANS 5:17–19, NIV

Prophecy of Isaiah

He is despised and rejected of men; a man of sorrows, and acquainted with grief: and we hid as it were our faces from him; he was despised, and we esteemed him not.

—ISAIAH 53:3

The word *despised* used in this verse means to look down on with contempt or aversion; to regard as worthless or distasteful.[1] Even though Jesus came to fulfill prophecy, the demonic conspiracy that sent Him to the cross has its roots in envy, jealousy, pride, and ignorance. It is easy to point fingers at any particular generation or people and blame them for rejecting the Messiah, but many today are still rejecting the free gift He came to offer. How often have we turned deaf ears to His call and plea? Any form of disobedience is an act of rejecting and despising Him.

Surely he took up our pain and bore our suffering, yet we considered him punished by God, stricken by him, and afflicted.

—ISAIAH 53:4, NIV

The suffering afflicted on Jesus is the price of redemption which every individual ought to have borne, but no human was pure enough to pay that price, let alone have the capability to endure the punishment.

The word *affliction* is a state of being *afflicted*, persistent pain or distress, great suffering agony, anguish, misery, torment, torture, travail, tribulation, or woe.[2] The movie *Passion of the Christ* gives us a visual idea of what Jesus endured. But as graphic as the movie is, it still does not come close to the actual affliction Jesus endured.

The apostle Peter made reference to Isaiah 53:5–6 in his Epistle: "Who his own self bare our sins in his own body on the tree that we, being dead to sins, should live unto righteousness: by whose stripes ye were healed" (1 Pet. 2:24).

Peter's emphasis is to affirm to the New Testament church the fulfillment of the prophecy of Isaiah. The punishment of Jesus is for our forgiveness and His wounds for our total healing: "For he hath made him to be sin for us, who knew no sin; that we might be made the righteousness of God in him" (2 Cor. 5:21).

This imputed righteousness mentioned here by the apostle is not one that any of us did anything to merit or earn. And our own righteousness is as filthy rags (Isa. 64:6).

> Some pour out gold from their bags and weigh out silver on the scales; they hire a goldsmith to make it into a god, and they bow down and worship it.
>
> —ISAIAH 46:6, NIV

A major problem globally today is poverty, but this problem or curse was solved in Jesus.

> For ye know the grace of our Lord Jesus Christ, that, though he was rich, yet for your sakes he became poor, that ye through his poverty might be rich
>
> —2 CORINTHIANS 8:9

The totality of our redemption was accomplished by and in Christ Jesus on the cross.

> Christ hath redeemed us from the curse of the law, being made a curse for us: for it is written, Cursed is every one that hangeth on a tree: That the blessing of Abraham might come on the Gentiles through Jesus Christ; that we might receive the promise of the Spirit through faith.
>
> —GALATIANS 3:13–14

There is no sin we could ever commit that the blood of Jesus does not have an answer to in forgiveness and the cleansing. The blood prevailed and broke the backbone of every sin and any curse.

> We all, like sheep, have gone astray, each of us has turned to our own way; and the LORD has laid on him the iniquity of us all. He was oppressed and afflicted, yet he did not open his mouth; he was led like a lamb to the slaughter, and as a sheep before its shearers is silent, so he did not open his mouth. By oppression and judgment he was taken away. Yet who of his generation

protested? For he was cut off from the land of the living; for the transgression of my people he was punished. He was assigned a grave with the wicked, and with the rich in his death, though he had done no violence, nor was any deceit in his mouth. Yet it was the LORD's will to crush him and cause him to suffer, and though the LORD makes his life an offering for sin, he will see his offspring and prolong his days, and the will of the LORD will prosper in his hand. After he has suffered, he will see the light of life and be satisfied; by his knowledge my righteous servant will justify many, and he will bear their iniquities. Therefore I will give him a portion among the great, and he will divide the spoils with the strong, because he poured out his life unto death, and was numbered with the transgressors. For he bore the sin of many, and made intercession for the transgressors.

—ISAIAH 53:6–12, NIV

Awesome prophecy!
Awesome words!
Awesome testimony!
Awesome accomplishment!

THE PERFECT SACRIFICE

No human vocabulary can explain in depth the awesome sacrifice of Jesus that broke the curse to set humanity free. Consider this revelation in the Book of Hebrews 9:11–12:

> But Christ being come an high priest of good things to come, by a greater and more perfect tabernacle, not made with hands, that is to say, not of this building; Neither by the blood of goats and calves, but by his own blood he entered in once into the holy place, having obtained eternal redemption for us.

The sin or iniquity that was and is the root cause of any curse was no match for the perfect sacrifice. As He hanged on the cross, having accomplished all that His father sent Him to do, Jesus declared, "It is finished!"

> When Jesus therefore had received the vinegar, he said, It is finished: and he bowed his head, and gave up the ghost.

—JOHN 19:30

Heaven and earth and all of creation waited for this hour to hear those three words from the lips of the Redeemer. By these words the kingdom of darkness was under divine arrest, as every sin since the first Adam was forever forgiven, the *curse of the law* was broken forever (Gal. 3:13). In his famous speech, "I Have a Dream," Martin Luther King Jr. probably had this hour in mind, among others, when he quoted the lyrics from the song by the same name written by J.W. Work, "Free at last, Free at last, Thank God almighty we are free at last."[3] Every drop of blood from the veins of Emmanuel (Jesus) was an answer to sin, iniquity, and the curse.

Jesus shed His blood in seven different places. He was led to be slaughtered as a lamb.

> He was oppressed, and he was afflicted, yet he opened not his mouth: he is brought as a lamb to the slaughter, and as a sheep before her shearers is dumb, so he openeth not his mouth.
>
> —ISAIAH 53:7

There are many schools of thought in reference to the seven places Jesus shed His blood. Some Bible scholars have added the blood Jesus shed during circumcision as a child. This action is recorded in Luke 2:21: "And when eight days were accomplished for the circumcising of the child, his name was called JESUS, which was so named of the angel before he was conceived in the womb."

A follow-up scripture would be Colossians 2:11: "In whom also ye are circumcised with the circumcision made without hands, in putting off the body of the sins of the flesh by the circumcision of Christ." For the purposes of our studies in the next chapter, however, we will limit it to the blood He shed during the week of His Passion.

*But He was wounded for our transgressions, He was bruised
for our guilt and iniquities; the chastisement [needful to obtain]
peace and well-being for us was upon Him, and with the stripes
[that wounded] Him we are healed and made whole.*
[Isaiah 53:5, amp]

Chapter 16

THE SEVEN PLACES JESUS SHED HIS BLOOD

1. In the Garden of Gethsemane

It was through His blood shed here that Jesus won back our will power.

> And being in agony he prayed more earnestly: and His sweat was
> as it were great drops of blood falling down to the ground.
>
> —LUKE 22:44

In the Garden of Eden, Adam used his will power to choose disobedience over God's revealed word to him. God created man as a free moral agent, and He gave him a will to make choices. Adam, by the choice of his will, sold the human race into bondage. The second Adam, Jesus, also entered a garden called Gethsemane, and by the exercise or choice of His will, obeyed God to win back our will power. By reason of what Jesus saw in the cup in the garden—the suffering, sin, iniquity, pain, etc.—His agony and travail in prayer was so intense, it opened up His pores to allow blood and sweat to flow freely. Medical doctors have confirmed this possibility under the circumstances of extreme stress in which Jesus found Himself.[1]

2. From the plucking of His beard

In 2 Samuel 10:1–5 and 1 Chronicles 19:3–5, the story is told of the mockery and shame that Hunan, son of Nahash, brought upon the servants of David who had been sent to him on a goodwill (ambassador) mission. David's response of advising the servants to seclude themselves until their beard grew back gives us insight into the Jewish mindset of the times.

> I offered my back to those who beat me, my cheeks to those who
> pulled out my beard; I did not hide my face from mocking and
> spitting. Because the Sovereign LORD helps me, I will not be

disgraced. Therefore have I set my face like flint, and I know I
will not be put to shame.

—ISAIAH 50:6–7, NIV

*The blood that poured forth as Jesus' beard was plucked broke the
curse of mockery and humiliation.*

When we die to self, we don't have to be ashamed anymore. Consider
how they treated Jesus:

> The high priest tore his clothes. "Why do we need any more wit-
> nesses?" he asked. "You have heard the blasphemy. What do you
> think?" They all condemned him as worthy of death. Then some
> began to spit at him; they blindfolded him, struck him with their
> fists, and said, "Prophesy!" And the guards took him and beat
> him.
>
> —MARK 14:63–65, NIV

3. From the stripes (wounds) on His back

Jesus' body (back) was flogged like a criminal until it no longer
resembled human flesh. The prophet of old foretold this incident seven
hundred years before it took place.

> Just as there were many who were appalled at him—his appear-
> ance was so disfigured beyond that of any human being and his
> form marred beyond human likeness—so he will sprinkle many
> nations, and kings will shut their mouths because of him. For
> what they were not told, they will see and what they have not
> heard, they will understand.
>
> —ISAIAH 52:14–15, NIV

> He grew up before him like a tender shoot, and like a root out
> of dry ground. He had no beauty or majesty to attract us to him,
> nothing in his appearance that we should desire him.
>
> —ISAIAH 53:2, NIV

Now look at how it went down two thousand years ago:

> Then released he [Pilate] Barabbas unto them: and when he had
> scourged Jesus, he delivered him to be crucified.
>
> —MATTHEW 27:26

The weapons used to flog Jesus' body mangled him till His blood poured forth. This is where the curse of sickness and disease was broken. Luke wrote in the Book of Acts,

> How God anointed Jesus of Nazareth with the Holy Ghost and with power: who went about doing good, and healing all that were oppressed of the devil; for God was with him.
>
> —ACTS 10:38

Sickness is an oppression of the devil, but that oppression of the oppressor was broken by Jesus' stripes.

Read the account of Peter:

> Who his own self bare our sins in his own body on the tree that we, being dead to sins, should live unto righteousness: by whose stripes ye were healed.
>
> —1 PETER 2:24

Every sickness ever known to man and released by the curse was broken forever. "Beloved, I wish above all things that thou mayest prosper and be in health, even as thy soul prospereth" (3 John 1:2).

The stripes and wounds of Jesus made Isaiah 33:24 possible. Oh, praise God! Turn to it, mark it in your Bible, say it out loud, and declare it boldly!

> And the inhabitant shall not say, I am sick: the people that dwell therein shall be forgiven their iniquity.
>
> —ISAIAH 33:24

Now read Isaiah 53:5 again and again.

> But he was pierced for our transgressions, he was crushed for our iniquities the punishment that brought us peace was on him, and by his wounds we are healed.
>
> —ISAIAH 53:5, NIV

I see you healed from today from every sickness and disease. Every sickness in your bloodline and those caused by curses, the curse is broken and you are healed in the mighty name of Jesus Christ.

4. From the crown of thorns pushed into His head

> To Adam he said, "Because you listened to your wife and ate fruit
> from the tree about which I commanded you, 'You must not eat
> from it,' Cursed is the ground because of you; through painful
> toil you will eat food from it all the days of your life. It will pro-
> duce thorns and thistles for you, and you will eat the plants of
> the field. By the sweat of your brow you will eat your food until
> you return to the ground, since from it you were taken; for dust
> you are and to dust you will return."
>
> —GENESIS 3:17–19, NIV

The disobedience of Adam brought a curse upon the ground. Adam
and Eve had everything they ever needed provided freely without
sweat. The curse affected the produce of the ground by yielding thorns
and thistles through sweat, struggle, and suffering.

*When the Roman soldiers twisted a crown of thorns taken from the
cursed ground and beat it onto the head and brow of Jesus, the curse
in the ground was broken guaranteeing the believer sweatless blessings.
The curse of poverty was broken.*

> And the soldiers platted a crown of thorns, and put it on his head,
> and they put on him a purple robe.
>
> —JOHN 19:2

Thorns are designed to inflect pain. In His parable of the Sower,
Jesus said: "And some fell among thorns; and the thorns sprung up,
and choked them" (Matt. 13:7). Jesus taught that thorns have the
ability to outgrow good seed and choke the life out of it.

I see every choking ability of thorns in your life and bloodline
broken and destroyed as you continue in obedience to God's Word.
May the works of your hands be blessed in Jesus' name!

5. From the nails in His hands

*The blood that poured out of Jesus' nail-pierced hands bought back
our inheritance.*

> They pierced my hands and my feet.
>
> —PSALM 22:16

Blotting out the handwriting of ordinances that was against us, which was contrary to us, and took it out of the way, nailing it to his cross; And having spoiled principalities and powers, he made a shew of them openly, triumphing over them in it.

—COLOSSIANS 2:14–15

6. From the nails in His feet

The nails that pierced Jesus' feet bought back our peace, restoring the dominion and authority lost in garden.

Jesus gave us the great commission, a commission that requires exercising dominion and authority over all the works of the enemy (see Matthew 28:19).

There are several places in the world today that will not accept the gospel unless they see a demonstration of the power of God. As witnesses of the Lord Jesus, we must produce the evidence of His resurrection.

Verily I say unto you, Whatsoever ye shall bind on earth shall be bound in heaven, and whatsoever ye shall loose on earth shall be loosed in heaven.

—MATTHEW 18:18

And my speech and my preaching was not with enticing words of man's wisdom, but in demonstration of the Spirit and of power.

—1 CORINTHIANS 2:4

And your feet shod with the preparation of the gospel of peace.

—EPHESIANS 6:15

Arise and take your place in the army of the Lord! March with authority into the devil's camp and take back what he stole from you. Take it all back, beginning with your immediate family. You can do it in Jesus' name!

7. When Roman soldier pierced His side

One of the soldiers pierced Jesus' side with a spear, bringing a sudden flow of blood and water.

—JOHN 19:34, NIV

The Roman spear that pierced the side of Jesus also crushed his heart, allowing water and blood to gush out. Remember Jesus went to the cross to do a divine exchange. By allowing his heart to be crushed and broken, He made provision for our broken and wounded hearts.

Before going to the cross, He gathered his friends to tell them about issues of the heart.

> But the things that come out of a person's mouth come from the heart, and these defile them. For out of the heart come evil thoughts—murder, adultery, sexual immorality, theft, false testimony, slander.
> —MATTHEW 15:18–19, NIV

The Flood of Noah came because of the conditions of man's heart.

> Then the LORD saw that the wickedness of man was great in the earth, and that every intent of the thoughts of his heart was only evil continually.
> —GENESIS 6:5, NKJV

The plague of the heart is deep and wide. The Bible says the heart is desperately wicked.

> Not a word from their mouth can be trusted; their heart is filled with malice. Their throat is an open grave; with their tongues they tell lies.
> —PSALM 5:9, NIV

> The heart is deceitful above all things, and desperately wicked: who can know it? I the LORD search the heart, I try the reins, even to give every man according to his ways, and according to the fruit of his doings.
> —JEREMIAH 17:9–10

When Jesus sacrificed His heart for us, He knew this would be the only way to reconcile man back to Himself.

As Charles Hutchinson Gabriel wrote in his song, "I Stand Amazed," "How marvelous how wonderful, Is my Saviour's love for me."

The piercing was prophesied before He was born.

> And I will pour on the house of David and on the inhabitants
> of Jerusalem the Spirit of grace and supplication; then they will
> look on Me whom they pierced. Yes, they will mourn for Him as
> one mourns for his only son, and grieve for Him as one grieves
> for a firstborn.
> —ZECHARIAH 12:10, NKJV

The blood of Jesus is our fortress. It is endowed with power to free
every prisoner of hope from the waterless pit:

> As for you, because of the blood of my covenant with you, I will
> free your prisoners from the waterless pit. Return to your for-
> tress, you prisoners of hope; even now I announce that I will
> restore twice as much to you.
> —ZECHARIAH 9:11–12, NIV

It is time to lay hold of the stronghold of the blood to free every
prisoner in your bloodline who is under any curse. Read verse 12
again; it says, *"Even now I announce that I will restore twice as much
to you"* (NIV, emphasis added).

JESUS, THE CURSE BREAKER

> Then said I, Lo, I come: in the volume of the book it is written
> of me.
> —PSALM 40:7

Jesus came to fulfill what was written of Him in the volume of the
book. Part of that was to break the curse and restore humanity back
to God's original intent.

He put a stamp of approval on the prophecy of Isaiah 61:1 when He
affirmed it of Himself and demonstrated it in Luke 4:18:

> The Spirit of the LORD is upon Me, Because He has anointed Me To
> preach the gospel to the poor; He has sent Me to heal the broken-
> hearted, To proclaim liberty to the captives And recovery of sight
> to the blind, To set at liberty those who are oppressed.
> —LUKE 4:18, NKJV

He had a deliverance ministry that delivered everyone He encoun-
tered bound by the devil. Under the law, leprosy was considered a

curse. Those who contacted this dangerous disease were considered unclean. They became outcasts and had to announce their presence everywhere they went. Jesus, the curse breaker, mingled with lepers and healed them.

> A man with leprosy came to him and begged him on his knees, "If you are willing, you can make me clean." Jesus was indignant. He reached out his hand and touched the man. "I am willing," he said. "Be clean!" Immediately the leprosy left him and he was cleansed.
> —MARK 1:40–42, NIV

He demonstrated His love by reaching out to all with compassion.

> When he saw the crowds, he had compassion on them, because they were harassed and helpless, like sheep without a shepherd.
> —MATTHEW 9:36, NIV

The same compassion is available to you and your loved ones (bloodline) today. You don't have to suffer under any curse anymore. Rise up and take authority over every generational curse plaguing your bloodline!

> Behold, I give unto you power to tread on serpents and scorpions, and over all the power of the enemy: and nothing shall by any means hurt you.
> —LUKE 10:19

Matthew 16:19 tells us that whatever we allow on earth is what heaven will allow and whatsoever we disallow is what heaven will disallow.

> Simon Peter replied, You are the Christ, the Son of the living God. Then Jesus answered him, Blessed (happy fortunate, and to be envied) are you, Simon Bar-Jonah. For flesh and blood [men] have not revealed this to you, but My Father Who is in heaven. And I tell you, you are Peter [Greek, Petros—a large piece of rock], and on this rock [Greek, petra—a huge rock like Gibraltar] I will build My church, and the gates of Hades (the powers of the infernal region) shall not overpower it [or be strong to its detriment or hold out against it]. I will give you the keys of

the kingdom of heaven; and whatever you bind (declare to be improper and unlawful) on earth must be what is already bound in heaven; and whatever you loose (declare lawful) on earth must be what is already loosed in heaven.

—MATTHEW 16:16–19, AMP

HOW TO COOPERATE

Obedience

Obedience is the master key to walking in the blessings after the curse is broken. Obedience is a requirement if you are going to experience the blessing of the Lord. It was a requirement under the law and it is a requirement now.

> If you fully obey the LORD your God and carefully follow all his commands I give you today, the LORD your God will set you high above all the nations on earth.
> —DEUTERONOMY 28:1, NIV

> Now if you obey me fully and keep my covenant, then out of all nations you will be my treasured possession. Although the whole earth is mine.
> —EXODUS 19:5, NIV

We are in the dispensation of grace, and obedience is still the requirement.

> If you keep My commandments, you will abide in My love, just as I have kept My Father's commandments and abide in His love.
> —JOHN 15:10, NKJV

> You are My friends if you do whatever I command you.
> —JOHN 15:14, NKJV

The Holy Spirit

The Holy Spirit came as our helper. Jesus said He (the Holy Spirit) will teach and guide us.

> But the Advocate, the Holy Spirit, whom the Father will send in my name, will teach you all things and will remind you of everything I have said to you.
> —JOHN 14:26, NIV

Won't you invite Him in now? The Holy Spirit will give you the power and grace to walk in obedience to God.

> And I will put my spirit within you, and cause you to walk in my statutes, and ye shall keep my judgments, and do them.
>
> —Ezekiel 36:27

Engage prayer

When breaking curses, your prayer has to be effectual and fervent, a prayer of faith.

> Is anyone among you in trouble? Let them pray. Is anyone happy? Let them sing songs of praise. Is anyone among you sick? Let them call the elders of the church to pray over them and anoint them with oil in the name of the Lord. And the prayer offered in faith will make the sick person well; the Lord will raise them up. If they have sinned, they will be forgiven. Therefore confess your sins to each other and pray for each other so that you may be healed. The prayer of a righteous person is powerful and effective.
>
> —James 5:13–16, niv

The Archbishop Duncan Williams said, "Consistent and persistent prayer produces permanent results."[2] It is not so much what you say in prayer, but it is more your attitude, approach, and the condition of your heart. Jesus spent quality time with His Father in prayer. Apostle Paul summed up the prayer ministry of Jesus in the Book of Hebrews:

> During the days of Jesus' life on earth, he offered up prayers and petitions with fervent cries and tears to the one who could save him from death, and he was heard because of his reverent sub-mission. Son though he was, he learned obedience from what he suffered and, once made perfect, he became the source of eternal salvation for all who obey him.
>
> —Hebrews 5:7–9, niv

Humility

Walk also in humility and totally submit yourself to God.

> Likewise, ye younger, submit yourselves unto the elder. Yea, all of you be subject one to another, and be clothed with humility: for

God resisteth the proud, and giveth grace to the humble. Humble yourselves therefore under the mighty hand of God, that he may exalt you in due time.

—1 PETER 5:5–6

Mercy and thanksgiving

Let us therefore come boldly to the throne of grace that we may obtain mercy and find grace to help in time of need.

—HEBREWS 4:16, NKJV

God has never turned away from the sincere cry for mercy for His mercy endures forever. Read the entire chapter of Psalm 136.

We need to be appreciative and thankful as a recipient of God's mercy.

The Bible says,

In every thing give thanks: for this is the will of God in Christ Jesus concerning you.

—1 THESSALONIANS 5:18

And they overcame him by the blood of the Lamb and by the word of their testimony, and they did not love their lives to the death.
[Revelation 12:11, nkjv]

Moreover David said, "The Lord, who delivered me from the paw of the lion and from the paw of the bear, He will deliver me from the hand of this Philistine." And Saul said to David, "Go, and the Lord be with you!"
[1 Samuel 17:37, nkjv]

Chapter 17
TESTIMONIES

*And they overcame him by the blood of the Lamb, and by the word
of their testimony; and they loved not their lives unto the death.*
—REVELATION **12:11**

L ET THESE TESTIMONIES be a source of encouragement to you as
well as provoke you to rise up and begin to break every curse
over your life.

DELIVERANCE OF A VILLAGE

My parents were born in a particular village in Ghana where the norm
of the day was strong occult, fetishes, and witchcraft. Many from this
village and surrounding villages struggled to rise and live a normal
comfortable life. Nothing seemed to prosper. Even the local river that
the villages fished out off dried up periodically.

In my early years as a young minister, the Lord used me to bring
revival to this village trough the preaching of the gospel. After the
conversion of my mum to Christianity, her transformation sparked
a revival in the village. Many turned to the Lord and brought out
their idols to be burned publicly as they renounced their old ways.
The curse and spell over the village was broken, giving way to infrastructure and the building of roads, schools, churches, electricity, and
in recent times by the Grace of God, the discovery of many natural
resources including oil. Though one may argue that these developments are part of a growing economy, it is well stated in scripture that
sin is a reproach to any people. And the fact remains that the curse
was broken and these villages have become centers of commerce with
resorts for vacationers.

RAISING THE DEAD

I grew up on a suburb of Accra in Ghana. In the late '70s this region suffered much retrogression where nothing prospered nor made headway. This regression included a few orthodox churches that had become more of a formality. Very few attended service and that was out of obligation. Most people seem to operate under the spell of two men in the region who were strongholds. They bewitched this region with the spirit of divination and sorcery, and many feared them. Every morning before the dawn of day, they were up performing rituals to appease the idols that were erected in their compounds. I knew this because this was the time when I also went out to preach in the streets. For several years I watched people turn away from my preaching to consult with these men.

One morning one of them lost his oldest son, who died suddenly. His gods failed to bring him back to life. He fed the idols with animal blood, poured some concoction on them while invoking the names and spirits of dead ancestors, and he did the ritual dance, all to no avail. Just like Baal who failed his prophets on Mount Carmel, his gods failed him. The news spread very quickly and most of the people who lived in this suburb gathered in his compound due to the much wailing, weeping, and chanting. An entire day had passed since the young man died.

I was returning home from a prayer retreat when I came upon the scene. Someone in the crowd shouted, "The preacher is here! Let him also call on his God!" And with that I was led into the room where the dead body lay. It was a small room erected with fresh palm branches to house the deceased. I closed the door behind me and began to speak in tongues (my prayer language).

After a while, drenched with sweat and discerning no sign of life, my mind began to recollect the scripture where Jesus took the hand of the little girl in Mark 5:41 and said, "Talitha cumi,... I say unto thee arise." I thought that was the name of the little girl. I walked back to the dead body, shouted his name out loud, and repeated the words of Jesus, "I say unto you arise!" Suddenly I felt movement in my hands as he that was dead sneezed, opened his eyes, and looked at me with a confused gaze.

This sweeping move of the Holy Spirit broke the spell and curse of retrogression over this region. Churches began to spring up and flourish. The man and his family gave their lives to Christ and joined the Foursquare gospel church. The young man attended Bible school and served in ministry for many years until the Lord called him home into glory. Infrastructure and new developments in this suburb took a turn for the better. Oh, how powerful is the gospel of Jesus Christ that liberates the captives of any spell and curse!

RAIN IN DRAUGHT SEASON

Several years ago I was introduced to a glorious family where I met my future wife. The entire family served God faithfully. Her mum started a fellowship that eventually produced many great men and women of God who went out to champion the cause of the gospel in the country and all over the diaspora. We realize as the fellowship grew that most of the people came from outside the neighborhood.

There was a strongman who resisted the gospel in this region. There was also a spell of widespread witchcraft in this region. It was common to see people rise up early in life and then lose everything. During the summer of 1981 a strong draught hit the city. The lack of rain and intense heat caused many bush fires.

One afternoon, as my friends and I preached in the streets, I felt inspired by the Holy Spirit to declare a downpour of heavy rain about the same time the following day. Upon hearing the news, my future mother-in-law, who is now with the Lord, locked herself up in prayer, as was her custom to stand in the gap. Together with the rest of the family, we waited on the Lord to confirm our words with a notable miracle. About the same time the following day, the crowd gathered and many were there to make mockery of us as they have done in the past. At exactly twelve noon, without any clouds or lighting or thundering or strong wind, the heavens opened and poured out much rain.

The curse and spell of witchcraft was broken as people from the neighborhood flocked into the fellowship. The gospel has the power to break any curse and spell. And your town, city, or neighborhood could be next.

FRUIT OF THE WOMB

When the Lord moved us into Houston, we started a church that became known as the church of fruitfulness. We saw the curse on the fruit of the womb broken off of many married couples. People came from all walks of life to be recipients of this grace and miracle. We had a woman in her fifties take seed of triplets. Several women under this curse gave birth to twins. All to the glory of God!

KENNEDY TRAGEDIES

Many families across the nations of the world can identify with the tragedies that befell Joseph and Rose Kennedy and their relatives, particularly their children and grandchildren.[1] One can only hope that the snare and curse is broken and subsequent generations are no longer victims and captives for this dark shadow called a curse.

You and your bloodline don't have to be victims such as these. Knowledge has been made available. Arise, get up from where you are with the knowledge that you've received and run into the battle in the name of Jesus and let the devil know enough is enough, no more. Break every curse over your bloodline through the power and the blood of Jesus Christ.

NOW, YOUR TESTIMONY

As I travel the nations of the world proclaiming the gospel, I have come into places dedicated to idol gods. Sometimes it was difficult seeing the stranglehold of these gods over the region and the evidence of the numerous curses they brought to its inhabitants. I've seen idol gods and shrines erected at both the entry and exit boarders of some of these places. In fact, some of these towns and villages have been named after these gods.

The god of this world, Satan—the devil, has blinded the understanding of many from seeing and hearing the truth of the gospel that could set them free. One of the curses he has used effectively in these regions is poverty. Poverty is a curse of the worst kind. The Bible says that a poor man's voice is not heard and his wisdom is despised.

This wisdom have I seen also under the sun, and it seemed great unto me: There was a little city, and few men within it; and there came a great king against it, and besieged it, and built great bulwarks against it: Now there was found in it a poor wise man, and he by his wisdom delivered the city; yet no man remembered that same poor man. Then said I, Wisdom is better than strength: nevertheless the poor man's wisdom is despised, and his words are not heard.

—ECCLESIASTES 9:13–16

For the earnest expectation of the creature waiteth for the manifestation of the sons of God. For the creature was made subject to vanity, not willingly, but by reason of him who hath subjected the same in hope, Because the creature itself also shall be delivered from the bondage of corruption into the glorious liberty of the children of God. For we know that the whole creation groaneth and travaileth in pain together until now.

—ROMANS 8:19–22

I want to suggest to you that you are a great man and woman of valor and God wants to use you to accomplish the great mission of a deliverer to bring your family name out of obscurity.

Time and again I watched the sustainable hand of the Lord as He disarmed darkness, breaking spells and curses to liberate all mankind. Your testimony is next, because "greater is he that is in you, than he that is in the world" (1 John 4:4). God wants to use you to break the curses over your village, town, and city. He wants to give you a testimony as a deliverer in your region for His glory. God is waiting on you, and your region is also waiting on you. Will you accept His call? Great grace awaits you even now.

Shall the prey be taken from the mighty, or the lawful captives of the just be delivered? For thus says the Lord: Even the captives of the mighty will be taken away, and the prey of the terrible will be delivered; for I will contend with him who contends with you, and I will give safety to your children and ease them.
[Isaiah 49:24–25, AMP]

Chapter 18
DECLARATIVE PRAYER

ONSIDER THESE SCRIPTURES as we go into a prayer of agreement together. On the basis of the blood of atonement, get rid of any fear and come before the throne of God boldly in prayer.

> Let us then approach God's throne of grace with confidence, so that we may receive mercy and find grace to help us in our time of need.
> —HEBREWS 4:16, NIV

> But the righteous are bold as a lion.
> —PROVERBS 28:1B

Gather your family and begin to declare these prayers over them, as I declare it over you.

> [The Lord] Who confirms the word of His servant and performs the counsel of His messengers, Who says of Jerusalem, She shall [again] be inhabited, and of the cities of Judah, They shall [again] be built, and I will raise up their ruins.
> —ISAIAH 44:26, AMP

According to Matthew 18:19, "If two of you on earth agree about anything they ask for, it will be done for them by my Father in heaven" (NIV).

> *I come into agreement with you to break every curse that has held you captive in the mighty name of Jesus Christ. The curse is broken, and I command a divine arrest of every enforcer of curses in your bloodline.*
> *Your appointment with early death is cancelled. By the grace and mercy of God your appointment with curses by authority figures is broken and cancelled. Your appointment with curses of seedtime and harvesttime is broken*

and cancelled. *Your appointment with curses from sexual escapades, idolatry, lies, and deadly words is broken and cancelled. Your appointment with curses from your generational and ancestral background is broken and cancelled. Your appointment with slander, defeat, divorce, chronic sickness and diseases, poverty, destruction, negative stigma, satanic and demonic harassment, miscarriage, misrepresentation, inferiority complex, satanic snares, snare of the fowler, shame, reproach, accidents, sorrow, satanic surprises, witchcraft, pain, vexation, demonic intimidation, borrowing, torment, demonic manipulation, satanic domination, loneliness, guilt, fear, offence, spiritual ignorance, denials, near-success syndrome, disregard, disfavor, strange children, early death, the grave, agitations, satanic conspiracies is broken. Your appointment with all the above is broken and cancelled in the name of Jesus Christ.*

By the power of the blood of the eternal covenant, I come into agreement with you to break every curse of financial drought and limitation placed upon the works of your hands. I revoke the curse of non-achievement. In the name of Jesus, I command every embargo and stronghold of the enemy over your testimony to be broken even now!

Arise! Arise! Like a mighty warrior, shake off every dust of defeat and despair. Go forth a conqueror for the glory of God in the mighty name of Yeshua HaMashiach, Jesus the Christ, Son of the living God. Amen.

I declare:

If the Son therefore shall make you free, ye shall be free indeed.

—John 8:36

NOTES

CHAPTER 2
OPERATIONAL MEDIUM OF A CURSE

1. *Dictionary.com*, s.v. "curse," http://dictionary.reference.com/browse/curse?s=t (accessed August 18, 2014).

2. Derek Prince, *Blessings and Curses* (Grand Rapids, MI: Chosen Books, 2003).

3. George Hartwell, "What Is a Curse? Definition of a Curse," *Listening Prayer.com*, http://listening-prayer.com/curses/what%20is%20a%20curse.html (accessed August 18, 2014).

4. Ibid.

CHAPTER 3
THE CURSE OF GOD

1. Duncan Williams, "known in many parts of the world as the 'Apostle of Strategic Prayer' and is the Presiding Archbishop and General Overseer of Christian Action Faith Ministries (CAFM). CAFM has over 150 affiliate and branch churches located in North America, Europe, Asia and Africa. Archbishop Duncan-Williams is also the Founder and President of Prayer Summit International," http://www.awclaurel.org/ab-nicholas-duncan-williams (accessed August 19, 2014).

CHAPTER 4
THE CURSE OF SEEDTIME AND HARVEST

1. Mike Murdock, *Wisdom Commentary*, vol. 1 (Denton, TX: Wisdom Center, 2002).

CHAPTER 5
THE CURSES OF ANGER, RESENTMENT, AND BITTERNESS

1. Williams.

2. Dwight Thompson, interview by Rod Parsley, *Praise the Lord*, Trinity Broadcasting Network, March 13, 2014, http://trinitybroadcastingnetwork.info/trinity-broadcasting-network/men-of-god-talk-about-forgivenes (accessed August 19, 2014).

3. Ambrose Bierce, "Ambrose Bierce Quotes," *Goodreads, Inc.*, http://www.goodreads.com/quotes/9909-speak-when-you-are-angry-and-you-will-make-the (accessed August 19, 2014).

4. Anonymous, "Anger Quotes," *Notable Quotes*, http://www.notable-quotes.com/a/anger_quotes.html (accessed August 19, 2014).

5. Virgil Aeneid, "Virgil Quotes," *Notable Quotes*, www.notable-quotes.com/v/virgil_quotes.html (accessed August 19, 2014).

6. Maya Angelou, *BrainyQuote*, http://www.brainyquote.com/quotes/quotes/m/mayaangelo148635.html (accessed August 19, 2014).

7.   Daniel Webster, *BrainyQuote*, www.brainyquote.com/quotes/quotes/d/danielwebs379808.html (accessed August 19, 2014).

8.   John Webster, "Anger," *Quote Cosmos*, www.quotecosmos.com/quotes/2547/view (accessed August 19, 2014).

Chapter 6
The Curse of Authority Figures

1.   Michael Pitts (Cornerstone Church, Toledo, OH), spoken at the Annual Impact Conference in Ghana, West Africa, December 2010.

Chapter 7
The Curse of Gossip

1.   Noah Webster, *Webster's New International Dictionary* (London: 1913), s.v. "gossip," http://machaut.uchicago.edu/?resource=Webster%27s&word=gossip&use1913=on (accessed August 19, 2014).

2.   *Wordnet Dictionary*, s.v. "gossip," http://wordnet-online.freedicts.com/definition?word=gossip (accessed August 19, 2014).

3.   Michael Wheeler, "Avoiding the Dangers of Gossip" (February 15, 2010), *Articlesbase.com*, http://www.articlesbase.com/leadership-articles/avoiding-the-dangers-of-gossip-1863065.html (accessed August 19, 2014).

Chapter 8
Generational Curses

1.   Williams.

2.   Paul Hewett, *Conceptual Physics*, 2nd ed. (Upper Saddle River, NJ: Prentice Hall, 1992), 28.

Chapter 10
Innocent, Ignorant, or Deliberate Acts That Invoke Curses

1.   *Merriam-Webster Dictionary*, s.v. "coups d'état," http://www.merriam-webster.com/dictionary/coup%20d'%C3%A9tat (accessed August 19, 2014).

2.   Mike Murdoch, *101 Wisdom Keys* (Ft. Worth, TX: The Wisdom Center, 1994).

Chapter 12
Sexual Doorway

1.   *Mnemonic Dictionary*, s.v. "cleave," http://mnemonicdictionary.com/word/cleave (accessed August 21, 2014).

Chapter 13
Destructive Words

1.   "The Romans Destroy the Temple at Jerusalem, 70 AD," *EyeWitness to History* (2005), http://www.eyewitnesstohistory.com/jewishtemple.htm (accessed August 21, 2014), and, Steve Rudd, "Flavius Josephus Describes the

Destruction of Jerusalem," *Bible.ca*, http://www.bible.ca/pre-flavius-josephus-70AD-Mt24-fulfilled.htm (accessed August 21, 2014).

    2.   William Shakespeare, *The Tragedy of Julius Caesar*, act 3, scene 2, line 1619.

CHAPTER 14
SHEDDING INNOCENT BLOOD

    1.   *History of Africa Otherwise*, "Fiji: the Repentance of a Cannibal Village," blog entry by Kanyarwunga, October 9, 2011, http://historyofafrica otherwise.blogspot.com/2011/10/fiji-repentance-of-cannibal-village.html (accessed August 21, 2014).

CHAPTER 15
LET THE HEALING BEGIN

    1.   *Merriam-Webster Dictionary*, s.v. "despise," http://www.merriam-webster.com/dictionary/despise (accessed August 19, 2014).

    2.   *Merriam-Webster Dictionary*, s.v. "affliction," http://www.merriam-webster.com/dictionary/affliction (accessed August 19, 2014).

    3.   Martin Luther King Jr., *I Have a Dream: Writings and Speeches that Changed the World* (San Francisco: Harper, 1992), 106.

CHAPTER 16
THE SEVEN PLACES JESUS SHED HIS BLOOD

    1.   H. R. Jerajani, et al., "Hematohidrosis: A Rare Clinical Phenomenon," *Indian Journal of Dermatology* 54.3 (July–September 2009), 290–292, http://www.ncbi.nlm.nih.gov/pmc/articles/PMC2810702/ (accessed August 22, 2014).

    2.   Williams.

CHAPTER 17
TESTIMONIES

    1.   Beth Rowen, "Timeline of Kennedy Tragedies," *Fact Monster*, © 2000–2014 Pearson Education, publishing as Fact Monster, www.factmonster.com/spot/kennedytimeline.html (accessed August 18, 2014).

ABOUT THE AUTHOR

DR. AUGUSTINE DEGORL is the senior pastor and founder of Throne Room Worship Center in Houston, Texas. Throne Room is the home to a multicultural, nondenominational congregation that is making a difference within the community and affecting many lives worldwide.

With the Word of God so richly in his mouth, Degorl has proclaimed the gospel and served in ministry for over thirty years, including Action Chapel International, fulfilling various ministerial and pastoral duties. He has served as the PR and armor bearer to general overseer, presiding Archbishop Duncan-Williams, also known as the Apostle of Strategic Prayer. His affiliation with the archbishop, who also is his spiritual father and mentor, has greatly impacted his prayer life and ministry.

Augustine Degorl earned his doctorate from Tabernacle Bible College and Seminary and his commission is in accordance with Isaiah 58:12: to build up the old waste places and raise up the foundations of many generations, to be a repairer of the breach and restorer of paths to dwell in.

This is being accomplished through his passion and apostolic anointing for the power of prayer and healing. Degorl has the grace to communicate scriptures with simplicity and understanding. Preaching the gospel has taken him around the world. His charismatic personality and profound revelation has him sought after literally all over the world including Africa, Asia, Europe, South America, the Caribbean, and the U.S. The major portion of his ministry is focused on various areas of prayer strategies, healing, and deliverance.

He has been married to his lovely wife, Pat, for over twenty-two years, and they are blessed with two lovely children.

CONTACT THE AUTHOR

Website:
www.augustinedegorlministries.org

Email:
augustinedegorl@att.net

Address:
Throne Room Church
2703 Highway 6 South Ste 145
Houston Texas 77082

Phone:
281-589-8722